Perfect
People
Skills

Perfect People Skills

ALL YOU NEED
TO GET IT RIGHT
FIRST TIME

ANDREW FLOYER ACLAND

ARROW
BUSINESS BOOKS

Published by Arrow Books in 1997

1 3 5 7 9 10 8 6 4 2

© Andrew Floyer Acland 1997

Andrew Floyer Acland has asserted his rights under the Copyright,
Designs and Patents Act, 1988 to be identified as the author of this work.

First published by
Arrow Books Limited
20 Vauxhall Bridge Road, London SW1V 2SA

Random House Australia (Pty) Limited
16 Dalmore Drive, Scoresby, Victoria 3179, Australia

Random House New Zealand Limited
18 Poland Road, Glenfield
Auckland 10, New Zealand

Random House South Africa (Pty) Limited
Endulini, 5a Jubilee Road, Parktown 2193, South Africa

Papers used by Random House UK Limited are natural, recyclable
products made from wood grown in sustainable forests. The
manufacturing processes conform to the environmental regulations
of the country of origin.

Companies, institutions and other organizations wishing to make bulk
purchases of any business books published by Rantom House should
contact their local bookstore or Random House Direct:
Special Sales Director
Random House
20 Vauxhall Bridge Road
London SW1V 2SA
Tel: 0171 840 8470 Fax: 0171 828 6681

Random House UK Limited Reg. No. 954009
ISBN 0 09 979601 5

Set in Bembo by
SX Composing DTP, Rayleigh, Essex
Printed and bound in Great Britain by
Cox & Wyman Ltd., Reading, Berkshire

CONTENTS

INTRODUCTION

On my first day in my first management job, the boss took me aside for a quick pep talk.

'Don't worry about the budget,' she said, *'it'll mostly take care of itself.'* She was wrong; and I learned a lot about managing budgets over the next few years.

'Get your diary and your time sorted out.' she said, *'and your life will be easy.'* She was wrong about that too; and only when I became self-employed did I really learn about time and its umbilical connection to money.

'It's the people problems which are always the worst,' she said. And boy, was she right about that. But she didn't have a clue how to solve them and neither did I. We made a great team.

Ten years down the road, I can say as we all do, I wish I had known then what I know now. It might not have made all the difference all the time, but it would have made some of the difference quite a lot of the time.

This little book is about the things which can make that difference. It is not about complicated management disciplines, or obscure personnel functions. It is not about setting pay levels to maximize incentive and minimize absenteeism; or how to set up structured appraisal schemes which, however good the intentions, always seem to have everybody shaking in their shoes.

It is really about the basic courtesies of living and working with other human beings – the things which became lost in the greedy 80s, and have been obscured by the shallow fashions of the 90s. It is about the behaviour which has been downsized and outplaced rather as those words are used to disguise the twin brutalities of overwork and redundancy.

I sometimes think we have made our lives so unnecessarily complicated by forgetting some basic qualities. As Robert Fulghum put it so perfectly:

> Most of what I really need to know about how to live, and what to do, and how to be, I learned in kindergarten. Wisdom was not at the top of the graduate school mountain, but there in the sandbox at nursery school. These are the things I learned: share everything; play fair; don't hit people; put things back where you found them; clean up your own mess; don't take things that aren't yours; say you're sorry when you hurt somebody; wash your hands before you eat . . .[1]

Because we seem to have lost such lessons, words like courtesy sound old-fashioned and idealistic – especially when our newspapers confront us with five-year-olds terrorizing their teachers and people being killed for tooting their car horns. But my dictionary defines courtesy as graceful politeness or considerateness in intercourse with others, which sounds pretty good to me, whether the year is 1890, 1990, or 2090.

But of course it isn't quite this easy, is it? Because what do you do if your graceful politeness is perceived as weakness, or condescension, and the response is contempt, rudeness, or even violence. And that is just the beginning, because as much as one might regret the passing of more courteous times, they also disguised some subtle forms of manipulation and exploitation.

We are caught in a kind of trap. Old ways of behaviour, rooted in dishonesty as well as deference, are no longer what we seem to expect or want, while ideas such as assertiveness and empowerment, which are arguably their

---

[1] *Everything I Need to Know I Learned in Kindergarten*
(Villard, New York, 1989)

replacements, can seem somewhat soulless even when used with the best intentions.

So the purpose of this book is really to remind us of the basic skills which make the difference between building relationships with people – and merely co-existing. This is my selection of the key people skills, and it may well be different from yours. Perhaps you will even find them idiosyncratic. I have, for example, omitted leadership and assertiveness, even though both of them are important skills, because so much has been written about them.

I hope you will find the ideas here timeless: as much carrying some perennial values as grounded in the realities of late-twentieth century life. While they are couched in the language of today – melding ideas from both management science, communications and humanistic therapy – they also reflect the importance of things earlier generations would have approved: self-discipline, responsibility and common sense.

There is nothing revolutionary about any of them. In fact, they are all things which, as Fulghum has it, should be taught in primary school and bred into the bloodstream of every home and organization. These are simple things like learning to listen and negotiate what you want, ask good questions and offer warm counsel.

Who should read it? I would say it is for anyone who values their relations with others, whether in the office, in the home, or in the world at large. It may also be useful for teachers and trainers who want some ideas for training courses or human relations classes. It offers both some general ideas and some specific points you may find useful.

The layout is as simple as it can be. Each chapter focuses on a particular skill. It is introduced in general terms, discussed, illustrated and explored, and the chapter closes with some ideas for how that skill can be developed, and finally a summary of the key points.

Running lightly through it, and I hope making it slightly different from similar presentations of interpersonal skills, are responses to the problem I mentioned earlier: what happens when other people seem not to respond to your people skills. Or, to put it more bluntly: what on earth we can do about the people we find *difficult*.

For me, this has enlivened the whole challenge of identifying the essential people skills. I have had to ask myself exactly how it is I do (or don't) cope with the people who refuse to melt in the face of my daunting charm, who overlook my intellectual gifts, who are not persuaded by my silver tongue. The answers have not been entirely reassuring, and the book is therefore something of a journey through the possibilities. Unlike the brave people who have an answer for every one of life's problems, I tend to think the journey is as important as the arrival.

Andrew Acland
Wotton-under-Edge
July 1996

GROUNDING

'I hate victims who respect their executioners'

Jean-Paul Sartre (trans.)

INTRODUCTION

In all the consultancy, mediation and training work I ever do there comes a time when people start asking *'But what do you do if someone is really difficult? If they just refuse to see another point of view? If they are totally irrational?'*

This is a crunch point, because we all know that some people are just, well, *difficult.* If you hear the usual talk about communication skills, and the need to be assertive rather than aggressive, and how to prepare for difficult meetings, don't you find yourself thinking *'Yes, but . . .'* or *'It's all very well, but . . .'?*

Relationships which work are not a problem. It does not take perfect skills to deal with the people we get on with easily and naturally. Our ordinary, everyday people skills will do fine most of the time. Oh, sure, we make mistakes, we unintentionally rub people up the wrong way, we say the wrong thing and have to apologize later. These are all part of being human and fallible, and there is nothing more boring than those who delight in pointing out such lapses. Most of the time our people skills are, to borrow a phrase which has passed into the common language of psychology, *good enough.* But sometimes good enough is *not* good enough.

The purpose of this book is to look at people skills particularly in relation to their value in dealing with the people we find difficult. You will not find difficult people featuring on every page or even in every chapter – but they are lurking in the background. Whenever I have had to choose what to leave out and what to include, it has always been with one eye on the difficult people.

This forces a degree of realism and also a point of departure which you should bear in mind throughout what follows – some people are almost impossible to deal with. I see no value in denying this. So let me declare here, straight out, *'Yes, there are some people who are extremely difficult and frankly you can do everything in this or any other book and still get nowhere with them.'* There are no sure-fire, fail-safe guaranteed ways to solve your people problems.

The bottom line is that you do your best and if it isn't good enough, go home, cuddle the kids (or your partner or the cat or someone, for heaven's sake) – and forget about it. If necessary move house, get a new job, emigrate, because there are limits to what most of us can achieve with the really difficult people, and if you start to fret over it you'll break your heart.

GETTING STARTED

The starting point is not, however, the difficult people. It is you. When it comes to your relationships with other people, and with yourself, are you a villain or a victim? Do you bully other people? Do you bully yourself? Have you bought this book because you want to get on better with other people? Or because you are fed up with being a victim of other people's *lack* of people skills?

To be honest, it doesn't much matter which, because villainy and victimhood are merely different stops on the same cycle. (Victims become villains to escape from being victims; villains become victims as their victims fight back.) If you want to understand the cycle more fully, I recommend Eric Berne's famous book *Games People Play.*[2]

---

[2] *Games People Play* by Eric Berne (Ballantine, 1978)

HOW NOT TO BE A VICTIM

Before you start improving your people skills you must first get out of the villain/victim role So let's get down to work by looking at how not to be a victim.

The first point to make is that there is quite a narrow line between being a victim and victimizing others. It's really a question of whether you take your frustrations out on others – or on yourself. It is the victimizing of others which makes you into a villain; the victimizing of yourself which prevents you dealing effectively with people – and may lead them to victimize you as well.

It is surprisingly easy to become a victim. The following exercise looks at ways in which all of us can begin to *believe* ourselves to be victims without noticing what we are doing.

Exercise: How to be a victim

Look through the following situations. Are any of them familiar?

- Losing your temper with frustration at some inevitable bureaucratic process
- Cursing and kicking your car when it does not start
- Holding a grudge and searching for an opportunity to remind someone of a past mistake
- Blaming a small child or an animal for not understanding something
- Replaying over and over in your mind a situation which you could have handled better
- Trying to do a DIY task with the wrong tool

Think about these. Who was the victim? Got it in one.

We usually turn ourselves into victims because:
- We blame someone or something else for our own shortcomings, and blaming others, especially unjustly,

has a way of backfiring
- We allow pride and ego to come between us and the actions we really need to take
- We put insufficient time and concentration into really understanding the demands which different situations make on us

GROUNDING – ESCAPING THE CYCLE

The first Perfect People Skill is being able to *ground* and *centre* yourself: because it is how you escape being either villain or victim. By being grounded and centred, you know who you are, and what you can and should do. You have no need to victimize others or yourself. It gives you the strength to look people firmly in the eye, say what you mean and mean what you say.

The following six steps will keep you grounded.

1. Accept due responsibility

This is the starting point both to not being a victim and to beginning to deal with other people effectively. We often go to great lengths to pass the buck and we need to be aware of the tricks we use to do it.

For example, we try to deny our responsibility. A probation officer friend once told me about a criminal who was on trial for stabbing someone to death. '*He fell on my knife,*' claimed the murderer. '*Really?*' she said, '*Nineteen times?*'
Taking responsibility for your own behaviour and the choices we make can be among the hardest of lifelong lessons. It is so easy to blame those endless, anonymous 'others' for what we think, what we believe, what we do. After a recent motorway accident in which many people died, some of the survivors were interviewed on television. '*It was the fog*' said one man. So the fog compelled people to drive into each other? Or is it more likely that people were driving too fast and too close together?

2. Choose how you feel

Are we responsible for the way we feel? When we are in love we delight in ownership of our meandering thoughts. When our thoughts are less pleasant we tend to shrug them off and say we are not responsible for the way we feel. How convenient.

If you victimize yourself with destructive introspection, the first step out of it is to recognize that you are doing so, and to spear the thoughts as they flit through your mind. Both the skill development exercises at the end of this chapter will help you with this. The combination of *mindfulness* – being aware of your own internal thoughts and images – and being prepared to challenge them can break the cycle of victimhood.

3. Broaden your perceptions

It is very easy to view the world through a mental periscope and steel blinkers from deep within your own little bunker. Do that for long enough, and you will begin not to notice just how limited those views are; how constrained your perceptions of the world have become. Soon you will only understand the world which you see from this limited viewpoint, and it will become very frightening because you will not be able to make sense of what you see. With fear will come hostility to everything which is unfamiliar – and fear and hostility fuel the villain/victim cycle.

Open your eyes and absorb as many and as intense impressions of the world as you can. Enjoy it in all its vigour and complexity.

4. Get your ego on your side

Someone I know, the director of a voluntary organization, is reviled by many of his peers, being accused of megalomania, power-hunger, manipulation. In truth, he has much to be proud of. Raised in a relatively deprived home in a poor country, he has worked his way to the top of a fine organization, and his efforts have expanded its staff and its budget many times. He deserves to be admired: he has earned the right to an inflated ego.

But an inflated ego can make it difficult to see what is apparent to others. It is already happening with this person. I have seen him cut off the person talking to him because someone more important has turned up. His body language betrays the kind of self-importance which is off-putting and even offensive. There are beginning to be whispers against him, enumerations of his vanities and weaknesses, distrust of the achievements he claims.

He is a victim of his own ego. It has given him the strength to get where he is; now he needs to learn the humility which is a characteristic of all truly great people.

5. Concentrate

It is easy to blame the car for not working when we need it to. Or to rage against the interest on a credit card bill because we have failed to pay it on time. Or to shred the vital screw because we could not be bothered to use the right screwdriver.

A lot of the villain/victim cycle stems from *carelessness* – literally from lack of care about what we do and how we do it. Taking time to maintain the car; taking care to pay the bill on time; concentrating on the needs of the job in hand and not thinking about half a dozen other things: these are the simple, obvious things which prevent disappointment and failure.

6. Don't take yourself too seriously

In the great scheme of things, most of our personal failings do not matter very much, and you can bet that you are much more conscious of your failings than most of those around you. Be ready to laugh with others and at yourself

There are so many things which should be taken seriously, for example: poverty and crime and child abuse, the torture of prisoners and the degradation of the environment. These are things we should get worked up about; these are the things which produce real victims. Laugh at yourself and care about the things which really matter – that's the motorway out of self-inflicted victimhood. As the actress Ethel Barrymore put it, *'You grow up the day you have the first real laugh – at yourself.'*

THE MOMENT OF CHOICE

We live in a reactive world. Much of what governments, businesses, or we as individuals do is shaped and determined by others.

Governments react to the perceived intentions of other governments, or to what the opinion polls are telling them, or what the newspapers said this morning. Businesses react to what their market researchers say the customers want, or to what their competitors are doing, or to the latest business craze – because businesses are as susceptible as teenagers to the tyrannies of fashion.

We as individuals spend much of our time reacting to those around us: to the behaviour of bosses, subordinates, colleagues, families and friends; to the powerful forces which so subtly mould what we think, eat and wear; how we spend our time, our money and how we live our lives. Most of the time we live reactive lives without realizing it, and feel a spark of envy when we read about someone who has defied convention to sail alone around the world, start a yak farm, follow their dream and succeed against all the odds.

The ease and habit of reaction obscure the element of *choice* in how we behave, and it is the matter of choice which is at the heart of this book. Faced with other people it is even more tempting to be reactive, to feel compelled to respond in a certain way: *'If he attacks me I have to attack him back –*

that's just the way I am.' The mark of the victim is not having a choice.

It doesn't have to be like this. Much of what we conveniently feel to be compulsion *is* actually choice — choosing to avoid cost, risk, loneliness, or responsibility. Our habits of reactive thinking blind us to the element of choice in so much of what we like to think is inevitable or uncontrollable. One of the worst effects of other people — if we do not have the skills with which to communicate and cope with them — is that they seem to deny us choice.

And this is where we come to the final point of this chapter. Other people will always stimulate a certain response from us — true. But between that stimulus and our response *there is a moment of choice*. It may be only for a heartbeat, but a moment nonetheless.

This is the moment in which we choose to be victims or villains, or we choose to break the cycle.

SKILL DEVELOPMENT

This is a lifetime's task: it is the work of growing and maturing as an individual, learning to have confidence in your own judgment, discovering sources of strength within and outside of yourself. There are two small, everyday things you can do to assist this process.

Both these exercises require you to make some time for them every day. You don't have any spare time? Poor victim. I bet you have time to watch television or go to the pub or read the newspaper.

This is choosing to use some of your time — perhaps just twenty minutes a day — differently. Try getting up earlier and doing both of these while the house is still quiet. The first hour of the morning is often the best of the day for doing this kind of work.

Exercise 1: Being still

You have to learn to be still and be silent if you are to feel grounded and centred. Take time (twenty minutes) every day to sit quietly and review where you are and what you are doing. If you want you can enhance this process by taking a course in meditation or by going on some kind of retreat. But those are extras: the first step is the discipline of taking time to be still and listen to yourself.

Exercise 2: Keeping a journal or diary

I have often noticed that people who keep diaries or journals seem to have a strong sense of themselves. It may be that putting your thoughts onto the page in a regular way makes sense of them, shows you when you are becoming obsessed, highlights the dangers of self-pity and self-indulgence. It is perhaps another form of meditation and being still.[3]

Summary

Avoid being a victim by being centred and grounded:

- Accept due responsibility
- Choose how you feel
- Broaden your perceptions
- Get your ego on your side
- Concentrate
- Don't take yourself too seriously

Develop these by taking time to:

- Be still
- Keep a journal or diary

---

[3] For a powerful introduction to the value of writing things down, I recommend *The Artist's Way* by Julia Cameron (Pan, 1995). You don't have to be an aspiring artist to profit from it.

2

LISTENING

> 'Definition of a bore: *A person who talks when you wish him to listen*'
>
> **Ambrose Bierce**

INTRODUCTION

What is listening? *What is* . . . You cannot be serious! Listening is what we all do all the time! We listen to the radio; we listen to the TV; we listen to our children, our partners, our parents, our bosses, customers, colleagues. We spend our lives listening. Or do we?

I don't think we do – perhaps because I spend quite a lot of my time sorting out the messes which people make when they do not listen. So what are they doing all that time when their ears are open and other people are making noises at them?

I'll tell you what they are doing. They are thinking about what they are going to say when it is their turn to speak. They are wondering what is for lunch. They are remembering something they have to do before the weekend. They are *hearing* what is being said to them, but they are not really paying attention to it. And because they are not really paying attention, the other person is beginning to feel frustrated, and so tries harder, and therefore puts their point more strongly. Which makes the person who is supposed to be listening begin to resent this ear-bashing they are getting, and concentrate even harder on what they are going to say when they get the chance. And because the person speaking feels that chance approaching, they get even more desperate to . . . You get the drift.

Why is simply listening and paying attention to people such

a challenge? Perhaps it is because we are so bombarded by noise and distraction these days that we unconsciously filter out most of what comes at us. Our modern terror of silence means that we are losing the discipline and the skill of giving our full attention to others. Remember the two simple exercises set in the first chapter, to help you ground and centre yourself – being still and keeping some kind of journal in which you note down what happens, and what you say to yourself? That is *internal* listening. Now we need to develop the habit and skill of listening *outside* ourselves: listening to others – especially to the others we find difficult.

WHY LISTENING IS IMPORTANT

There is something good which comes out of the lack of real listening. It means that when you do listen, *really listen*, to someone, the experience will be so novel and so special for them, you will have a friend for life. I know this, because as I was writing this book, a letter arrived from someone in America with whom I had one conversation two years ago. They were writing to recall that conversation and how much it had helped them on their way. What did I do to deserve such a letter? I listened.

The point was made more amusingly (and less piously – I don't usually include testimonials in my writing, but the timing seemed so perfect I could not resist it: perhaps synchronicity should be another people skill) by a colleague. When he was first introduced to listening as a skill, he was quite sceptical about its alleged power. He found himself with half an hour before a meeting one evening, and decided to practise this so-called 'skill'.

He went into a pub, sat at the bar, and got into conversation with someone. He listened, deliberately contributing nothing to the conversation, merely summarizing, paraphrasing and feeding back what the other person said to him – the active listening skills I will describe in a moment. When he finally got up to leave, the other person commented: *'Thank you. That is the most interesting conversation I have had for years.'* As Colin had done nothing other than feed back what he had heard, it tells you how important it is for people to *feel* that they have been listened to.

Why is it so important? Because few people really feel listened to these days. And because people do not feel others listen to them, they seek other ways of getting attention. Kids scrawl on walls; adults get drunk; malcontent managers spread rumour and innuendo; mischievous politicians rouse their followers to riot or march. The failure to listen, and to be listened to, is at the heart of many modern discontents.

When people are listened to they feel they *matter:* that what they think and feel is important. That they are important. And when people feel important (not *over*-important, because that leads to a whole other set of problems: but important enough to warrant attention) they feel responsible, and they act responsibly. This is why listening is important.

It is also important for a number of more prosaic and less drastic reasons:

- **Listening solves mutual problems:** it is ridiculous to disagree with someone until you understand their point of view.
- **Listening leads to cooperation:** when people reckon they are important to you, they will be more inclined to respect you in return and cooperate with you.
- **Listening helps your decision-making:** by listening to the experience and ideas of others you improve your own judgment.
- **Listening builds your own confidence:** the more you understand others, the more likely you are to do and say things to which they will respond positively.

- **Listening prevents conflict:** talking before listening leads to the foot-in-mouth experiences we never forget. You have two ears and one mouth: take the hint.

HOW TO LISTEN PROPERLY

The skills I am about to describe go under the general banner heading of *active listening*. Active rather than passive, I suppose, though I would prefer to think that proper listening can only be active listening.

There are four foundations of active listening: think of this as the **RASE** process for raising the quality of dialogue:

- **R – Responding to the content** (the subject matter of what is being said)
- **A – Acknowledging the feelings** underlying what is said
- **S – Showing you understand** and accept what is said
- **E – Encouraging further disclosure**

Let's look at these in turn.

- **Responding to the content**

The way you do this is by *paraphrasing* the content. Focus on the main subject of what is being said, and feed it back to the speaker. For example, someone says:

'The atmosphere at work is deteriorating daily.'

Your paraphrased response could be:

'So the situation is getting increasingly serious.'

This simple restatement tells the speaker you have understood the main point, and that you support their perception of the situation. (Note: their *perception* – this is not about judging whether they are right or wrong.

• Acknowledging the feelings

Then, you need to change your focus to the feelings behind what has been said:

'It sounds as if you are feeling very uncomfortable about what is going on.'

Acknowledging the emotional content of what is said – even if 'uncomfortable' is not quite the right word – lets them know their feelings are important and are being heard and understood.

• Showing you understand

The next step is to accept the legitimacy of those feelings, even if you do not agree with them:

'I can see how much you dislike working in the office when there is this tension in the air.'

You will find an overlap here when you reach the chapter on *empathy*: how there is a difference between sympathy – agreeing with what is felt – and simply accepting the fact of it without endorsing or rejecting it.

• Encouraging further disclosure

The final step in the **RASE** sequence is to get the person to tell you more by asking an *open question* (yes, that's the next chapter, 'Questioning'):

'Can you tell me a little more about what specifically is going on?'

You are now going for detail: I find that word 'specifically' one of the most useful in the language. Until you know something specifically, you don't really know anything.

Now, before you get carried away and think these four steps are the key to making friends and jazzing up your life, please do not think that listening begins and ends here. These are merely the foundations. Nor should you show off how well you listen – if you overdo these it will seem strained and unnatural to the speaker – these tools have to be used with some delicacy and, more importantly, with real sincerity. Fake sincerity provides the cringe factor in many TV send-ups of vicars and counsellors.

More active listening skills

So those are the foundations of proper listening, but there are a load more for you to practise.

1. **Shut up:** you cannot listen and talk at the same time (this is the hardest skill of all for some people to master).

2. **Be patient:** your gift of time and attention may be the most precious you ever make.

3. **Concentrate:** do not let your mind wander off on its own when the speaker says the same thing for the hundredth time. The content may be the same – but the small shifts in tone often tell you as much as the actual words.

4. **Leave your own feelings behind:** and please do not say *'I know how you feel'*, because in most situations you won't and cannot know how another person feels.

5. **Remove all distractions:** find a time when you can be alone, turn off the telephone, lock the door. Listening requires 100 per cent of your attention.

6. **Look at the speaker:** their posture and gestures will tell you as much about how they feel as what they say.

You will also notice if what they are saying is not matched by what their body is telling you – and it is the unconscious body movements which will be telling the truth.

7. **Make eye contact:** but do not stare them into sub-mission.

8. **Don't argue:** either mentally or directly. You may want to put across some different ideas, but leave this until you have finished listening and then ask questions.

9. **Listen for their personality:** the more you can discover about people personally, their likes and dislikes, motivations, ambitions and values, the better you can respond to them.

10. **Question your assumptions:** avoid making instant judgments based on whether you like their hairstyle or their taste in clothes; or putting them into boxes and stereotypes based on class, race or gender. And be aware of your own prejudices and how they may interfere with your listening.

SKILL DEVELOPMENT

How do you learn to listen? Mostly, you learn to listen by doing it, enjoying the results, and learning to do it even better next time. There are also a couple of exercises you can do with others.

Exercise 1: Accurate listening
Get into a group of three people.

Person A: puts a controversial point of view (abortion, capital punishment, nuclear power etc.; or something more fun like breeding penguins for food; turning motorways into organic vegetable gardens; making drug-taking compulsory) for about four minutes.

Person B: listens and, when **A** has finished, feeds back everything **A** has said. This is harder than it seems because your natural inclination is to be thinking all the time why **A** is quite wrong, not to say mad.

Person C: also listens, and when **B** has finished feeding back **A**'s arguments, asks **A** how accurate **B** was, and then initiates discussion about what might have got in the way of **B's** listening or feeding back accurately.

When that round is over, **Person B** becomes the speaker, **Person C** the listener and so on until everyone has had a turn in each role.

Exercise 2: Separating facts and feelings

People are always telling me that the *facts* are the key to every situation. In one sense they are right – until you have the facts you cannot make judgments or decisions. But the facts on their own are never enough, because people do not make judgments on facts alone, nor are they motivated by facts. People are moved and motivated by their *feelings* about the facts, their perceptions of the facts, their interpretations of the facts. Separate the facts from the feelings, and you begin to understand much more about a situation.

Get into a group of three people again.

Person A: talks for 3–5 minutes about something they really like or dislike doing: part of their job; something at home; some activity in which they have to take part on a regular basis.

Person B: listens for the facts in what the speaker says, while

Person C: listens for the feelings

When **Person A** has finished, **Person B** summarizes the facts without mentioning the feelings, and **Person C** feeds back the feelings without mentioning the facts.

Person A then comments on the accuracy of the listening, and on what it is like to have facts and feelings separated in this way. The others comment on how easy or difficult they found it to make the separation.

The roles then change and the exercise is repeated until each person has experienced each role.

It is always important to listen well, and listening to those people we find difficult is both harder and more important: because it is so easy to dismiss *what* they are saying because of *who* they are. Of course, they are victims of the cycle they create – they are difficult, people stop listening, they become more difficult trying to force people to listen. And so on.

Listening to the facts and feelings separately is a particularly good exercise to help you keep calm when dealing with a difficult person. In fact, it can help you to understand why they are difficult, because listening for their feelings forces you to appreciate their real motivation.

Summary
- **R**espond to what people say by summarizing and paraphrasing
- **A**cknowledge their feelings
- **S**how you understand and accept what is said
- **E**ncourage further disclosure

For even better listening:

- Shut up

- Be patient.
- Concentrate
- Leave your own feelings behind
- Remove all distractions
- Make eye contact
- Don't argue
- Listen for their personality
- Question your assumptions

Practise!

3

QUESTIONING

> 'Judge a man by his questions rather than by his answers'
>
> **Voltaire**

INTRODUCTION

There is a difference between merely asking questions, and asking questions which encourage people to make profound reappraisals of everything from their immediate behaviour to their understanding of life, the universe and everything.

When I was first training as a mediator and negotiator my tutor told me something I have always remembered. *'Don't say anything which hasn't got a question mark at the end of it. If you only remember halfway through that you should be asking questions rather than making statements, use your inflection to turn it into a question. If you get to the end and remember, tack on a question quickly. Statements generate resistance; questions generate answers.'*

He was right. Questions demand answers. Specific, well-crafted, searching questions which make us turn inward and pause before answering are also what make us move forward. When it comes to dealing with the people we find difficult, the question is both armour and weapon: it can save us from making statements which generate resistance; and it can tell us how to make progress.

ASKING QUESTIONS

Questions are usually divided into two types: the *closed*, which allows only 'yes' or 'no' answers; and the *open*, which produces new thought and information. For example:

'Did you remember to photocopy that report?'

– is a closed question.

'What have you photocopied today?'

– is an open question.

In a sense, all you need to know is that open questions are good for getting information, getting people to open up. Closed questions are good for verifying information and getting very limited, specific answers. As we live in an adversarial society, and we tend to think in terms of yes and no, right and wrong, black and white, I think we have a cultural tendency to use closed questions. Certainly if you listen to news programmes you will notice that journalists tend to ask closed questions, and then get upset when politicians refuse to give simplistic yes or no answers. For once I sympathize with the politicians.

To develop questioning as a distinct skill, however, we have to go beyond merely learning to ask open rather than closed questions. We need to begin to see questioning as a pattern, a sequence of focusing, rather like taking a series of photographs to make a photo-essay means taking a sequence of shots. Each picture has its own individual meaning and purpose, and when the whole lot are combined you have something which is more than the sum of the individual pictures. You have an entire story, a whole world captured.

Questions need to function in the same way, yet they have to be asked carefully and sensitively if the process is to be one of enlightenment rather than interrogation. Because this is the purpose of asking questions – literally, to shed light on their subject.

The Funnelling Down Technique
My first approach to asking questions is to use what I call the 'Funnelling Down technique'. The way this works is that you start with broad background questions and gradually make them narrower and more specific. Each of the five areas of question has a distinct purpose (in **bold** type):

1. Discover context
Questions about the background and context: *What's the story?*

2. Specify behaviour
Questions about specific behaviour: *Who did what?*

3. Query expectations
Questions about expectations: *What did you expect compared to what happened?*

4. Investigate motives
Questions about values: *What is important about this?*

5. Discover meaning
Questions about meaning for the individual: *What does this mean for you?*

As you can see, each of these five levels of questioning demands progressively more complex and detailed questions and answers. The purpose of using this technique is to:

- **focus** ever more closely on what really matters about the subject being investigated
- **clarify** exactly what happened, who did what and who thought what and what it all means
- **specify** particular details which may be significant
- **compare** what has happened or is happening to what people would prefer to happen
- **understand** the meaning of what has happened for those involved

Let us use the Funnelling Down technique to ask questions about a disastrous meeting in an organization. The person being questioned attended the meeting as an observer and occasional consultant to the organization. As a result of the meeting he is seriously thinking of resigning his role. These questions to him are designed to uncover as rapidly as possible what happened and how it affected him. This obviously has to be an extract from a lengthy conversation, so I have included one question from each of the five levels. In reality you would be asking several supplementary ones under each of those headings.

Q: What happened?
A: *The meeting was a disaster. For a start, the room was badly set up and the facilitator didn't seem to know what he was doing. There were no introductions, and the set-piece speech from the director set exactly the wrong tone.*

Q: What specifically did he do to set the wrong tone?
A: *He used a series of overheads to set out the organization's strategic plan.*

Q: What had you expected?
A: *Well, I had understood that the purpose of the meeting was to discuss the strategic plan, but he made it seem as if everything had already been decided.*

Q: Why is this difference important?
A: *Because part of the philosophy of the organization is that everyone should have the chance to contribute to deciding its direction. His approach seemed to violate the organization's basic values.*

Q: What is the significance of this for you personally?
A: *It makes me wonder whether I still want to spend my limited time working for this organization. I feel the association with it, if it continues like this, could damage my reputation.*

The Tunnelling Out Technique
You may remember from Chapter 1 about escaping from

victimhood that one of the remedies is to broaden your perceptions. It is also a way to help bump people out of their villainy, and the way to do it is by asking them questions which force them to expand their view of the world.

Where the Funnelling Down technique forces an increasingly narrow and specific focus for questions, the Tunnelling Out technique is designed to do exactly the opposite – to rescue people from their tunnel vision, free them from their blinkers, and help them to be more positive and optimistic about their ability to act in the situation. It is particularly useful to use with people who have become so focused on a problem that they are unable to see any way out of it.

1. Discover context
Questions about the problem:
What's the problem here?

2. Discover vision
Questions about ambitions: *What do you really want?*

3. Specify expectations
Questions to make the vision concrete: *How specifically will you know when you have what you want?*

4. Investigate resources
Questions to discover what resources are available to realize vision: *What skills, resources, expertise etc. do you already have which will help you achieve your vision?*

5. Broaden options
Questions to discover options already considered and to generate new ideas and perceptions about what might be possible: *What options are open to you? What else can you do? How else might you be able to achieve what you want?*

Let's return to our disgruntled consultant. He has stayed with the organization but is now frustrated because it does not seem to be going anywhere. He goes to the director and uses the Tunnelling Out technique:

Q: What is the problem with this organization? Why can't it move on?
A: *The real problem is that the staff do not work as a team.*

Q: What do you really want to achieve?
A: *I want the organization to work as one unit, able to respond quickly and flexibly to the opportunities in the field.*

Q: How specifically will you know when you have achieved this?
A: *We will halve the turnaround time on projects while at the same time expanding the range of work we do.*

Q: What skills, resources, and expertise do you already have which will help you achieve this vision?
A: *Well, one of our newest recruits is trained in matrix management, and I think that might solve our current limitations on capacity.*

Q: What else can you do?
A: *It may be that we could introduce a team-briefing system to improve communication and coordination . . .*

and so on.

HOW NOT TO ASK QUESTIONS

I have already mentioned some ways of questioning which may produce limited replies (such as closed questions) or resistance (when you cross the fine line between questioning and interrogation).

There are some other common mistakes people make when asking questions:

- **Asking too many questions**
  There is a certain television interviewer who regularly lets his victims off the hook because he cannot confine himself to one, well-crafted question. Instead he asks a whole series of questions at once, and the wriggling politician stops wriggling because all he or she has to do is answer the easiest, and then cannot even be accused of being evasive.

- **Asking leading questions**
  These are questions which either assume the answer, or which so constrain the answer that it will either seem evasive or downright implausible. The classic leading question, which I believe all trainee barristers are taught as an example of the genre, is: *'When did you stop beating your wife?'*

- **Asking intimate questions too soon**
  The closer your relationship with someone, the more intimate the questions you can ask. Ask too soon, and you will probably get a frosty reply. Try going up to someone you don't know at a party and asking about their sexual fantasies. Some may respond positively to this as an original opening gambit to a stranger; more may choose to slap your face. It takes all sorts.

  One of the challenges of dealing with difficult people is that we do not want to get close to them, and because of this we can rarely ask the questions they need to be asked (not just *'Why are you such a jerk?'*).

- **Asking questions at the wrong time**
  We have all seen the sad cliché of the television interviewer who goes up to the survivor of some tragedy and asks how they feel about their wife/husband/dog having been wiped out by the runaway train. That is an extreme example, however. By timing I really mean asking the right question at the right moment, which is

why the funnelling sequences of questions can be useful.

To get useful answers out of people, they have to be in the right state of mind to give them. So if you need to ask probing and difficult questions, spend some time listening to the person first, and allowing them to feel strong enough to handle the tricky questions.

HOW TO ASK QUESTIONS

That last point brings me to the matter of *how* to ask questions. As I mentioned above, people need to be in the right 'state' to answer questions, and if they are not you have to help them get into that state. Here are three steps you can take before asking the critical question to which you need an honest and constructive reply.

1. Ask several open, context-gathering questions.

2. Use active listening to show that you are absorbing the replies and are able to empathize with the person as they tell their story. When you have established some rapport by doing this –

3. Tell them you are about to ask a difficult question, and set them up to receive it. *'There is one particular question I need to ask you. I know you may find this difficult, so please do not feel that you have to answer at once . . .'*

Setting people up in this way reinforces their perception of your concern for their welfare, it reduces the shock of the question, and by allowing them space to reply you are more likely to get a considered response than a knee-jerk reaction.

SKILL DEVELOPMENT

Questioning, like listening, is one of the skills you can practise in everyday life. If you can make the opportunity to practise it deliberately, however, it is worth getting the funnelling and tunnelling sequences lodged in your mind. The following exercise can help this.

Exercise 1: The Funnelling Down Technique
Again, get into a group of three people.

Person A: outlines to **Person B** a situation or a problem which is troubling them.

Person B: asks five questions appropriately framed in the funnelling down sequence.

Person C: notes each question **Person B** asks.

When the five questions have been asked, **Persons A, B** and **C** comment on how much they have learned.

Persons B and C then ask a sequence of supplementary questions under each of the five headings, designed to build on **Person A**'s initial replies.

The purpose of this exercise is also to underline the value and productiveness of asking structured rather than random questions.

Exercise 2: The Tunnelling Out Technique
As above, only the questions are framed in the tunnelling out sequence, and designed to elicit new perceptions of the situation and options for resolving it.

Summary
Ask crafted and purposeful questions.

Funnelling Down to:
1. Discover context
2. Specify behaviour
3. Query expectations
4. Investigate motives
5. Discover meaning

Tunnelling Out to:
1. Discover context
2. Discover vision
3. Specify expectations
4. Investigate resources
5. Broaden options

To ask a difficult question:
1. Ask an open question to encourage disclosure
2. Listen carefully to build trust and rapport
3. Warn them that you are going to ask a difficult question, and prepare them for it.

4

EMPATHIZING

'Do not use a hatchet to remove a fly from your friend's forehead'

Chinese Proverb

INTRODUCTION

To find out how we affect others, and to be aware generally of what others are thinking and feeling, the skill we need is *empathy*. People often confuse empathy and sympathy, so let us begin by getting the difference clear.

Sympathy: is putting your arm around someone and commiserating with them: *'I am so sorry to hear about your cat being run over . . .'*

Empathy: is stepping into their shoes and understanding through painstaking listening and questioning exactly what it is they are feeling, what it is like to be them at this moment.

This chapter is not about empathy because it is somehow superior to sympathy. Sympathy, in its right place and expressed with sensitivity and compassion, is a vital quality, but being able to sympathize with someone is not a skill in quite the same way as empathizing. For me, empathy means that wonderful gift which some people have of making me feel that I am the most important person in the world, and yet at the same time being sufficiently objective to give me precisely the right advice. That combination of closeness and the clarity which comes with distance is what I aim for when I am trying to empathize.

THE IMPORTANCE OF EMPATHY[4]

Marooned on a desert island and only allowed to take one people skill, it would have to be empathy – even if there was nobody else around on whom to practise it. Of all the people skills, it is empathy which is the most fascinating to practise – as you will learn, I hope, if you do properly the long exercise at the end of this chapter.

Empathy is important because it enables us to understand how other people are: what makes them tick, how their worlds work, what matters to them. It is also through empathy, and empathy alone, that you will really find a way to deal with your difficult people. It may not always work – but at least you will have the satisfaction of knowing, if you have really used it, that nothing else would work: that you have done your best.

Empathizing with people you find difficult enables you to:
- See beyond stereotypes
- Read their maps
- Value your differences

EMPATHIZE TO SEE BEYOND STEREOTYPES

About the only thing that everybody has in common is that we are all different from each other. Perhaps it is this resultant complexity which encourages us to make the generalizations and lazy stereotypes of race (the stingy Jew; the conformist Japanese) and class (the effete aristocrat; the complacent bourgeois) and profession (the boring accountant; the bossy teacher), which so complicate our relations with others. The reality is, of course, that the differences between individual members of one such group are much greater than the overall differences between groups.

Other people are not the same as us, and stereotyping them

---

[4] For further and fascinating insight into empathy and much else, read *Emotional Intelligence* by Daniel Goleman (Bloomsbury, 1995)

is no substitute for understanding their different needs and interests, values and perspectives, education, training, experience. The more different from us they are, the more important it is that we should try to empathize with them in order to escape the stereotyping which, perhaps unconsciously, is one way we try to deal with difficult differences. Let me give you a personal example.

Some years ago I was involved in taking employers into schools in inner city areas. We arranged 'conferences' during which local managers and personnel officers would work with groups of children, talking about work, how to be interviewed, their hopes and ambitions. There were often moments of revelation for both sides. The kids discovered all sorts of things they did not know they could do – like stand up and make a presentation to the whole school. The employers learned to see through the stereotype of under-educated and unemployable 'problem' youth.

My moment of revelation came in a run-down school in Birmingham. It had been difficult to find local employers to participate because of the school's reputation. I was both pleased and mildly appalled to see a bank manager getting out of his car, complete with briefcase, shiny shoes, neat little bank-manager moustache. (Yes, I am still working on my prejudices.) I reckoned the kids would eat him alive.

The conference got under way. I went to check the groups. A couple of tough social workers in jeans and leather jackets were huddled in a corner, unable to get anywhere with their group. I moved on, now filled with fear and trepidation, to find out what these hulking yobs were doing to my precious bank manager. I found them sitting in neat rows scribbling furiously as he lectured them from the front of the room.

He had discerned what I, with my stereotypes in place, had

been unable to recognize: that what these kids wanted was someone to tell them how to get out of the slum into which they had been born. Of course they wanted to listen to him more than they would listen to social workers whom they would expect to confirm them in their place and role.

EMPATHIZE TO READ OTHERS' MAPS

When we see differences between ourselves and other people, we are not seeing them with unbiased eyes: we are seeing them through the filter of our own needs, values, experience and so on. In fact, we never see anything objectively, because **we do not see the world as it is – but as *we* are.**

We impose – project – upon it our own attitudes and beliefs, and these shape what we see. (In one of the quirks of the human psyche, we also tend to project the bits of ourselves we like least. So, for example, if I dislike a person because they are often angry, it may be because I recognize, and dislike, my own capacity for anger.)

This filtering, biasing, prejudicing and projecting process is unconscious and passive: we do not deliberately distort what we see, but somehow by the time it arrives it has undergone the distorting process. You see,

We see what we look for
(The old expression *seeing is believing* is quite the wrong way round)

and

What we look for is determined by what we believe it is possible for us to see.

Our beliefs form a kind of internal map of the world which we use to find our way. Just as a motorway map is a representation of the motorway network, so our internal map is a representation of the external world. The map is not the motorway; and our beliefs about the world are not the world – they are not 'true'. But we act as if they are – we have to, because without this internal map we would be as lost in the world as if we tried to drive without a map.

Another person, with different beliefs, will have a different map. If they are people of a different race, culture, or gender, then that too will affect the map they have. These different maps of the world are one of the major sources of tension and conflict between people. For example, when my wife and I drive across Europe we take two types of map. I take a European *through*-route map which shows the major roads and the fastest routes from Calais. My wife takes lots of large-scale maps which show the little medieval towns she likes to paint while I snooze in the sun. This works fine. Or, at least, it works providing we remember that we are working off different maps which have different scales and purposes. If we forget that, we end up lost, or very cross. *'That town does not exist'* I say. *'Well it does according to* my *map,'* she replies, *'and I want to go there!'*

The map is not 'real', but it is what we work from. So empathizing as a people skill is about discovering the maps which other people are using. Until you know what other people have on their internal maps, you really know too little either to understand them or to influence them. The people we call 'difficult' are those whose maps are most radically different from our own.

People have more than one map

People do not just have one map: they have several. When we have arrived at where we are going in Europe, I ditch the through-route map and use a local one for planning long walks. In the same way, I use a different map to plan my time at weekends than I do during the week. I use a different map when spending a day with my son than I do when working with a group of high-powered executives.

Sometimes I get my maps muddled. I get home from work and expect my son to have the insight and judgment of a hot-shot lawyer. Just occasionally I get it the other way round and treat the hot-shot lawyers like six-year-olds. (Sometimes that's no bad thing – six-year-olds know things which the rest of us tend to forget.)

Empathizing enables you to discern other peoples' maps, and to adjust your own in the light of them. Through empathizing you can build a relationship, and through that relationship you can show people other maps – your maps, which show your understanding of the world. Through this process it is sometimes possible, with time and care and skill, to change their in-built understandings of the world.

Can you really change people this way? Yes, because people change all the time anyway, as they learn and experience more, and adapt their maps accordingly. People can actually change quite fast if the need is there, for example:

- The person who has always 'known' themselves to be a coward, and then in a moment of crisis becomes a hero
- When different bits of map come together to form a new map, rather as your understanding of the jigsaw changes each time you add a new bit
- When your existing beliefs become so contradictory that you have to ditch the lot in favour of a new set

I think this last example explains why things like giving up smoking are so difficult. Not only do you have to work against the nicotine addiction, but you have to develop a new map of who you are. Going from 'smoker' to 'non-smoker' is enough to give anyone a map crisis.

EMPATHIZING WITH DIFFICULT PEOPLE
Very often the people we find difficult are those who have strong and very definite beliefs, because the stronger they

are, the harder it is to conceive that others may have different beliefs. Moreover, if those beliefs are all neatly combined into only one map – as they tend to be - then that person will find it quite difficult to understand anyone disagreeing with them.

The way we understand conflict with others rests on the way we understand our own internal conflicts and dilemmas. If we don't have any – because we just have this one all-singing, all-dancing perfect map – then of course we have no experience of arguing, negotiating and compromising with ourselves. We simply expect others to conform to our view.

The people we tend to find most difficult are those who seem unable to appreciate other points of view. They plough on regardless of others' objections because they believe everyone else is wrong. They have The Map. They must be right.

EMPATHIZE TO VALUE DIFFERENCES

Because our internal maps are so powerful, what we find 'difficult' in other people is often a reflection of 'difference'. When someone is very different to us, we may even describe them as 'irrational'. It's not a very useful description because all human behaviour is 'rational' in that it always has its own logic. The problem is that not everyone works to the same logic, and some people's logic is substantially different from our own. The answer is not simply to oppose or denigrate the logic of those we find 'irrational', but to find out how to merge our logic with theirs – and to do that you have to use empathy.

In any group of people, some will get on well together, and others less well. Our variations as human personalities guarantee that we will always find some people more difficult than others. The great value of being able to empathize is that it helps us to escape from the ghettos of our own making.

Differences need not become difficulties providing:

- We approach them in a spirit of curiosity and adventure
- We take time and effort to explore and understand them
- We value opportunities to perceive the world through new lenses
- We invest in building relationships to reduce projection and stereotyping
- We hold on to our own sense of purpose and identity

The more different you find another person, the more important that first skill of grounding and centreing yourself becomes if you are to be able to empathize effectively. The only people who suffer from culture shock are those who are not sufficiently rooted in their own identity to enjoy exploring others'.

Empathize with yourself

Do you bully yourself? If you do, it is likely you bully other people too. In fact, having asked yourself whether you are a victim, you should now ask yourself – *are you a villain?*

Think about the people you see on a daily basis. How do they respond to you? Do they bounce up to you with a spring in their step and a merry glint in their eyes? Or do they duck out of your way and pretend to have an urgent appointment along the corridor to avoid getting in the lift with you? What are you *really* like to be around? Take a good look in the mirror.

SKILL DEVELOPMENT

Exercise: Through the Looking-glass

Two advance health warnings: please take these seriously!

1. This exercise can be painful. If you do it on your own

you may end up depressed and scared by what it shows you. If you do it with someone else, it may reveal things you would prefer them not to know.

2. I strongly recommend that you do not go 'through the mirror' with your mother, an ex-partner, or anyone with whom you have had any kind of traumatic experience.

The purpose of this exercise is to experience how others experience you. I mean *experience*: this is not a casual navel-gazing exercise where you settle down with a drink for ten minutes of self-contemplation and emerge with a smug feeling that all is well in every department.

1. Sit down in a place where you meet others, especially those you find hardest to get along with. Select one of these people.

2. Make yourself feel how you usually feel when with this person. When you can do this, imagine them sitting in the room with you. Make your image of them as vivid as you can: their clothes, how they sit, their tone of voice, the expression on their face. Bring this person as vividly to life as you can. Describe this person to yourself or to the person with you. (If you are doing this on your own, you could try speaking into a tape recorder.)

3. Describe all your responses to this other person. What do you think of them? How do you feel when you are with them? How does your body react to them? Butterflies in the stomach? Sweaty palms? Notice everything and experience it as fully as you can. If imagining the other person in this way takes less than ten minutes it means you are cheating.

4. When you have this person and your reaction to them clear, stand up and shake off these impressions. Then

go to where you imagined them to be *and become them*. Take on their posture, their expression: take on everything you have just so vividly imagined about them. Become them as totally and as completely as you can.

5. When you know what it is to be this person, find out what it is like for them to be confronted with *you*. Now you have to imagine how you look to them, sitting behind your desk or in your armchair. Again, take plenty of time to do this. It won't work at once because it will take your poor brain some time to adjust to the shift, and at some level you may resist it.

6. When you have thoroughly experienced this other person's feelings in your presence, summarize what it is like to be this person, what is important to them, what they fear, what it is like for them to be faced with you. When you have done this, stand up, shake yourself down again, and move away from both positions.

7. Take another deep breath and a moment to settle down. From this detached position ask yourself:
   • What are the major differences between these two people?
   • What changes by which person would most help to bridge these differences?
   • What new resources of skill or understanding would help each person to make such changes?
   • How *specifically* should the first person (you!) respond to the other person when they next meet in order to change the relationship between them.

8. When you have spent some time being objective about yourself and the relationship you have with this other person, return to where you started and become yourself again. Now, recreate your image of the other person. How do you perceive them now? Do you respond to them differently from before?

9. When you have done that, shake yourself down, and become the other person again. How will they react when faced with your new approach? Test it out: become them and experience it. By this time you should be able to flit between being inside each person and experiencing their point of view. So continue to do it for as long as you can still learn.

10. When you have done enough, be sure to return to your own mind and body and settle back into them very thoroughly before you leave the exercise.

You may be surprised by how powerful and vivid an exercise it is to go through the looking-glass and see yourself through the eyes of others, and to enter their worlds. You might be surprised – and possibly alarmed that it is so easy to pull up the anchors of your normal identity. Do this often – in fact whenever you need to understand someone better – and you will soon be able to do it quickly and unconsciously with every person you come across. This is what the great empathizers do.

Summary
Empathy is the ability to experience fully the feelings and experience of another person. Empathy enables you to:
- Avoid stereotyping others
- Understand other people's maps of the world
- Value human differences

Practise it by going through the looking-glass with other people – especially with those you do not understand, or who seem to be scared of you.

5
SPEAKING

'If thought corrupts language, language can also corrupt thought'

George Orwell

INTRODUCTION

This chapter focuses on the process of communicating with words, whether spoken or written. While so much of modern communications is bound up with words, face to face with someone else, only a relatively small part of communication – perhaps less than 10 per cent – is actually carried by words and their meanings. The rest is carried by tone of voice and body language.

I always tell lawyers, who tend to do everything in writing, that it is their failure to use all the available means of communication which keeps them in business. They are sometimes surprised that about 90 per cent of mediation, which brings those in dispute to discuss their problems in person, is successful. Most of this is down to the mediator restoring effective human communication.

When it comes to dealing with other people, how we speak often determines:

- How well they understand us
- How well we relate to them
- How much we can influence them

This chapter describes some of what goes wrong with words, and some essential speaking skills to overcome the problems.

THE PROBLEM WITH WORDS

Have you ever had the feeling that although you have done your best to communicate something in words, somehow there are gaps in what you have said? Or that the full impact of some experience has got lost in the telling? Or that however carefully you have tried to explain something, your listeners have missed the vital point?

There is a real problem with words. However carefully we use them, they are always a *representation* of what we mean. The weakness of words is that they only provide a one-dimensional tool to convey our three-dimensional thoughts, emotions, experiences. Some of us get over the inadequacies of language better than others. The great poets and novelists, for example, become great precisely because they are able to use language which transcends its own limitations. They have only the same pathetic black squiggles on the page as the rest of us, and yet they can use them in a way which allows us to see and feel and hear what they describe.

One of the more recent systems for studying and understanding the limits of language goes under the forbidding name of Neuro-Linguistic Programming.[5] NLP provides, among other useful communication tools, a means to make language more accurate and avoid the black holes in communication. Its value is immense, particularly when working in situations or dealing with people where accurate communication is essential. Anybody seriously interested in increasing their people skills could do much worse than take a course in its fundamentals. This chapter describes one or two of NLP's basic ideas for improving the way we use words under the three key headings mentioned in the introduction.

---

[5] For a readable introduction to NLP try *Introducing Neuro-Linguistic Programming* by Joseph O'Connor and John Seymour (Mandala, 1990)

SPEAKING TO IMPROVE UNDERSTANDING

NLP's language tools are based on the observation that human language, in order to be functional, has to simplify the feelings or experiences it needs to convey. The three universal methods of simplification are:

Deletion: Language is selective in the experience it represents – a great deal has to be left out simply for communication to be possible.

Distortion: We simplify what we say because communication would otherwise be immeasurably tedious – but the process of simplification inevitably leads to distortion.

Generalization: We generalize in order to avoid spelling out every condition and exception.

These mechanisms are essential for fluent communication, and they also make certain activities possible: training and education, for example, would be impossible without generalization. The problems arise when people delete, distort and generalize *differently*. For example, something deleted by one person because it is regarded as irrelevant may be highly valued by the person to whom they are speaking.

NLP offers a sequence of questions designed to replace deleted information, reshape what has been distorted, and make specific what has been generalized. A word of warning: these linguistic devices are universal and deeply ingrained, and by challenging them you can be seen to be aggressive, pedantic, and intrusive. It is essential to question them indirectly and gently, using softening phrases such as '*I wonder . . .*' or '*I am curious to know how . . .*' It is also preferable to question language in this way once you already have some rapport with the other person, and once they know that their use of language is not being picked to pieces merely for your amusement.

Replacing Problem Language

NLP's general approach to resolving the misunderstandings caused by deletion, distortion and generalization is to ask for more specifics. So, for example, if someone says *'The organization is unhappy about this'* you would question it by asking *'Who, specifically, in the organization . . .?'*

Similarly, if someone uses an adverb to convey a judgment, as in *'This policy is clearly wrong'*, you would ask *'Clearly to whom?'* As you get more practised in spotting the problems caused by inadequate language, you begin to notice how often we use words such as *all, always, never, none, every.* These generalizations can be potent substitutes for thought and encouragements to mindless prejudice.

We also hamstring ourselves with our language. Words such as *cannot*, and *impossible* are used by people to deny capability, when what they are really seeking is to avoid choice, as for example when someone says *'I cannot do that'* when what they mean is *'I do not want to do that'*. The way to challenge this is *'What would happen if you did . . .'* or *'What stops you?'* On the same lines, words like *should, should not, ought, must* imply the existence of some set of rules and, again, they are mechanisms for limiting choice and behaviour. Challenge them by asking *'Who says?'* or *'What would happen if you did?'*

Among the more interesting of processes by which language corrupts thought is that of *nominalization.* This is the technical term for the interesting process by which verbs are turned into nouns, and in the course of it lose their meaning. A good example is 'education'. Unless one knows who is educating whom, about what, and how, the word is meaningless.

SPEAKING TO HELP BUILD RELATIONSHIPS

NLP studies language not simply to clear up communication problems, but also to help develop relationships. One of the ways it does this is to identify underlying patterns in a person's language so that you can then use the same language patterns when speaking to them. This helps to tell people that you understand the world the same way as they do.

Language Patterns

For example, I was once involved in the running of a conference on a tricky political situation. When I analysed the opening speeches of the leaders on each side, I was able to identify significant differences in the underlying language patterns. One side tended to describe the situation in terms of what they were trying to *move away from*, while the other side talked specifically about what they wanted to *move towards*. The differences of language resulting from this were continual and pronounced. I checked this with one of the delegates. *'Yes'* he said, *'It would be much easier to make progress if we knew what they wanted rather than what they do not want.'*

As somebody who is regularly involved in conflict as a mediator, I also notice that while some people habitually look for common ground, others always look for differences. Our adversarial culture tends to promote the latter, which may explain why lawyers, politicians and journalists tend to ignore areas of agreement and focus on areas of tension and dispute, even though they may be relatively minor.

Language patterns can be summed up as peoples' underlying preferences for a way of operating in the world. If you use the same patterns as another person – if you can manage it – it can be a powerful way to convey understanding of their map of the world.

51

Sense Preferences

NLP also suggests that people's thinking, remembering, communicating and experiencing have to be stored in one or more of the five human senses of sight, hearing, feeling, touch, taste and smell. These five senses provide the five *representational systems* through which experience is turned into language. People use all these systems all the time, but they tend to have preferences. An artist, for example, may tend to imagine things in pictures, whereas a musician may use sounds or a sculptor, touch.

These preferences can be apparent from the words which each of these individuals uses. The artist may use words which express a visual understanding (she may understand *clearly*, have a good *focus*), while the musician may express himself in terms of how things *sound*. Because we use language to code and communicate our thoughts, so the words we use reflect the way we think.

Not all language uses representational systems. For example, it is unusual to find this sort of sensory specific language in academic texts: it is too subjective. Instead there will be many sensorily 'neutral' words such as understand, interpret, perceive. One of the problems of sensorily-neutral words is that they do not force us to use our senses. This is why you and I sometimes leave lectures saying things like: *'I couldn't quite grasp his point'*, or, *'I didn't see what she was getting at'*.

Using the same sense words as another person tells them that you construct the world the same way they do – to use the language, you will see eye to eye, be on the same wavelength, or build a solid understanding. Sometimes it can be useful to 'translate' from one sense to another. If you think you are not understanding another person as well as you might, try to work out their sensory preference. If it is different from yours, try translating your language into the sense preferred by the other person. For example, your 'shared vision' for your organization may have to be translated into a 'harmonious programme' before it *sounds* good to some of your colleagues.

Manipulation?

NLP is widely regarded as a leading 'people skills' technology, but it is also quite controversial. Not only is there some debate about whether it works (NLP would say it may not be true but it can be useful to believe it is . . .), but there is also concern that it can be manipulative. Two answers are offered in reply to this.

First, NLP is simply making conscious what human beings do anyway. For example, when we say someone is charismatic or someone else has superb interpersonal skills, what we may be detecting is their natural ability to use some of the skills described here.[2] In other words, some people are naturally better at influencing us than others.

The second reply to criticism is that it depends on your intention in using them. If people develop these skills purely to advance their own interests (and NLP is now widely used, for example, in sales training) then it may well be used manipulatively. If you are using them to influence a dictator to behave more compassionately, then probably nobody is going to complain. Intention is everything.

SPEAKING TO INFLUENCE OTHERS

Speaking in public is apparently one of our most common nightmares. There you are, spotlit at the podium, and you have lost your notes, or you suddenly realize you are naked, or your speech bears no relation to the intended subject.

Public speaking is not just a technical skill, it is also a people skill, which is why it finds a place here. If you are interested in the technical bits – how to prepare, structuring a good speech and so on – I suggest you buy a specific book on the subject.[6] I am going to concentrate here on the human aspect, and this means talking about *states* and *rapport*.

NPL defines the *state* of a person as the sum of their physical and emotional condition at a particular moment. The main physical signs of state to observe are posture, and movements of their limbs and upper body. Your audience's state gives you vital verbal and non-verbal information about how you are doing. What I am about to tell you is terribly obvious, but I have listened to too many insensitive speakers to leave it out.

1. **Before you speak, observe your audience's general state.** Are they excited, restless, enthusiastic, asleep? Unless you know how they are, you cannot know whether your tone should be designed to wake them up or calm them down. You have already written and prepared your speech, so you cannot change the content very much, but you still have your tone of voice and your own body language to use appropriately.

2. **Throughout your speech, keep your eyes moving over the audience.** Aim to make eye contact, however fleeting, with every individual at least once during your speech, and watch for changes in your audience's state. If they are attentive to begin with (looking at you, heads slightly on one side to listen), and then you begin to see lots of upper-body movement, it means you are losing them.

3. **Just because you are at the podium and they are in the audience does not mean you cannot have a relationship with them.** Use all the senses: show pictures, tell stories, produce objects they can imagine

---

[6] In this same series there is *Perfect Presentation* by Andrew Leigh and Michael Maynard

feeling. Public speaking involves more than using words in public! Build *rapport* with your audience, and you will have influence with them.

4. **I define rapport as a state of deep empathy.** Rapport is particularly important if you need to challenge your audience. The stronger your relationship with someone, the more you can afford to confront or contradict them. It is the same with an audience. But once you have that rapport, be careful about losing it. If you are properly attuned, you should immediately notice any signs of resistance or incomprehension.

5. **There is one final aspect of rapport which all public speakers do well to bear in mind: rapport with yourself.** If you are out of rapport with yourself, (for example, because you do not really believe what you are saying), it becomes much more difficult to establish rapport with others. If, being out of rapport, you have to coerce yourself, then you will probably try to coerce your audience too. They will notice; they will not like it.

SKILL DEVELOPMENT

How on earth do you set about developing the skill of being conscious of language? It is in part a matter of training, part a matter of habit and practice. If you have no time or money for training, try the following exercise.

Exercise: Using language

Get into a group with two other people.

Person A: describes a recent holiday for about five minutes
Person B: listens for and notes sense preferences.
Person C: listens for and notes other language patterns.

Persons B and **C** then discuss what they have noted. Then:

Person B: describes a recent holiday, using a different sense preference to **Person A**, and trying to use different language patterns.

Person C: then follows on and does likewise.

When each person has had a turn in each role, and a range of sensory preferences and language patterns have been used, discuss the effect of hearing a story in a preference and pattern whch is not your own, and trying to use one which is unfamiliar.

This exercise will both make you more aware of how you use language, and give you an idea of what a difference the words you choose can make to your experience of conversation. Developing skills of this sort are really, at the end of the day, a matter of attention and practice.

Summary
Language matters. Look out for:
- deletions
- distortions
- generalizations
– which hinder effective communication.

Use people's own
- sense preferences
- language patterns
– to show you understand them.

When public speaking, do the same to build
- **rapport**
with your audience, and be aware of their
- **state**
so that you can change tack as soon as you need to.

6

NEGOTIATING

> *'Many of us think negotiating with a car salesman is worse than root canal work without Novocain'*
>
> **The Haggler's Handbook[7]**

INTRODUCTION

You probably think of negotiation as something only done by international politicians or trade union leaders around big tables covered in papers. Actually, they don't really do the negotiating around those tables. It is done in the loo between sessions, and over lunch, and in dark and smelly corridors where nobody can find them nattering to the enemy. Then they go back into the formal conference room and make speeches saying why the other side's arguments are a load of rubbish.

Negotiation is something we do all the time without realizing it. We negotiate with our partners, children, colleagues. Negotiating is what we do when we need to agree with other people despite our different interests or different points of view.

Awareness of the importance of negotiating as a human skill has increased enormously in the past few years. Amazingly, it was only a couple of years ago, for example, that negotiating became incorporated into the curriculum of legal training – and negotiation is surely something which lawyers do all the time. But for a long time people have tended to think that negotiation is one of those unteachable skills: you either have it by instinct or you don't.

---

[7] *The Haggler's Handbook* by Leonard Koren and Peter Goodman (Century Business, 1991)

In fact, while negotiation is perfectly teachable and the plethora of courses and institutions now offering it is a testimony to that, formal negotiation is still one of the more complicated skills to master, and there is some danger in over-simplifying it. But here we are concerned about negotiating as an everyday skill: something which happens all the time. And because it is used so frequently, getting it wrong – perhaps because you don't realize that you are negotiating – is all the more damaging.

IMPROVING NEGOTIATION AS A PEOPLE SKILL

There are four aspects of negotiation which tax our interpersonal skills:

- **Getting what we want** without alienating the other person
- **Choosing a strategy to use**
- **Making progress as painless as possible** and
- **Reaching a realistic and mutually acceptable agreement**

This chapter looks at ideas for effective negotiation while at the same time preserving relationships with our 'opponents' – the inverted commas because not every negotiation has to be a battle.

GETTING WHAT WE BOTH WANT

People often approach negotiation as a battle. Sometimes this is necessary: but you can pay a high price for an adversarial approach in terms of the relationship and the future. It is often better to approach negotiation as a joint problem-solving exercise in which the object is for everyone to do as well as possible. The more work which can be done jointly, the more likely this approach will prevail and produce the benefits of a 'win-win' outcome.

The opposite of the adversarial approach is sometimes assumed to be a 'cooperative' one, in which you have to sacrifice your own interests in the name of consensus. This is often unrealistic and undesirable. A 'non-adversarial' approach simply means starting from the standpoint that agreement is in the interests of both sides, and it is therefore more efficient to use a process which encourages agreement rather than disagreement. This is our starting point here.

People conventionally negotiate by taking up their respective *positions* and then trying to nudge towards each other by adopting and relinquishing new positions as they explore each other's flexibility – or lack of it. This approach works perfectly well in some simple situations, but it has disadvantages. For example, each move towards the other person depends on the expectation that the other person will reciprocate – and that means taking quite a risk. If people cannot take the risk, you end up with a power struggle as each side tries to coerce and manoeuvre the other into making concessions.

This 'positional' negotiation encourages bluff and counter-bluff, muscle-flexing, playing to the gallery, and all the strutting, posturing and power-playing we regularly see between employers and unions, in Northern Ireland, or within the European Union.

There is an alternative. It means seeing negotiating positions simply as the tips of icebergs on which each party plants its flag and poses for the camera. The position tells you much about their public ambitions, and what they say from it tells you what they want you to know. The problem is that this is not enough: you need to know what underlies their positions. What do they really want to achieve? Where does the bluff – if it is – end and the real purpose of their posturing begin? If the positions are incompatible, as they almost certainly are or there would be nothing to argue about, how can they be moved towards each other?

The answer is to look below the surface of the iceberg and see what is really going on:

- What are the *interests* which the positions represent,

and

- What are the *needs* which motivate their interests.

When you start digging beneath the surface for interests and needs, you begin to discover, as the diagram below indicates, that there are always some needs and interests which are common to both people.

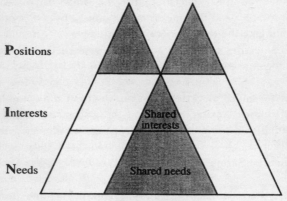

Positions

Interests

Shared interests

Needs

Shared needs

The P-I-N Triangle

These shared needs and interests are the common ground on which a mutually acceptable agreement can be built. This is only half the point, though. The crucial part is that **it is easier to move together from shared needs and interests than it is from incompatible positions.**

Shifting the focus from positions to needs and interests also bypasses the power struggle based on the need to control and dominate the other side by beating down their position. There are one or two more things to be said about this very simple concept.

1. **Interests and needs are not the same.** Interests tend to be things which people move towards because they give them pleasure. Needs, on the other hand, tend to be things, the absence of which people try to avoid because it causes pain. On the whole, interests *lead* while needs *drive*.

2. **Interests are always potentially negotiable; needs are, by definition, not negotiable.** If something is negotiable, then it is not a need. Conflict tends to bring needs to the surface: people suddenly discover the need to 'stand on their rights' or 'be heard' or 'demand that the authorities pay attention'. Needs can be repressed or suppressed – but they never go away.

3. **Both needs and interests can be material or abstract.** This is a particularly important point to remember when differences in values come to the fore.

Environmental conflicts provide interesting examples of value struggles. Until environmental and ecological issues became more widely understood from the 1960s onwards, a concern for conservation could probably have been described as an interest. As people's awareness of environmental issues has grown, however, and volunteers for organizations such as Greenpeace have become prepared to risk their very lives in defence of whales, for example, it is now probably true to say that conservation is felt by them to be an absolute need. Part of the gulf between business and environmentalists derives from the difference between environmentalism *perceived* as an interest to be negotiated with other interests, and environmentalism *felt* as an absolute and non-negotiable need.

So the overall point here is that to get what you want, it makes sense to help the other person get what they want too – and to start with this public intention from the outset.

CHOOSING A STRATEGY

Not every negotiation can be concluded on a 'win–win' basis. Sometimes you have to choose one of several possible strategies, and not all of them will lead to mutually acceptable outcomes.

The following graph sets out five possible negotiation strategies.[8] All of these have their uses, and the following paragraphs set out when you might choose one rather than another.

ASSERTIVE

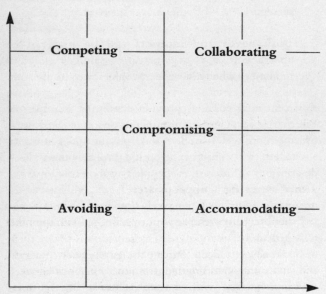

COOPERATIVE

---

[8] This is widely used in the negotiation field, but I don't know who conceived it. Due credit to them.

None of these five strategies is right or wrong, better or worse than the others. It is a case of determining which strategy is most *appropriate* to the particular circumstances.

Competing

Competing with the other side can become confrontational and aggressive: it means you are pursuing your own interests regardless of those of the other person. You use whatever power you have – position, money, charisma, intelligence – to defend and advance your position.

Competing is appropriate:

- when you need to protect yourself against people who are ruthless
- when you know you are in the right and can demonstrate it
- when there is no possibility of a consensual agreement

Compromising

Negotiation virtually always involves compromise: the question is whether you are forced into compromise through competition and confrontation, or whether you achieve it through a more cooperative approach. Compromising is usually realistic and may be perfectly satisfactory; but it may give you less than the optimum.

Compromising is appropriate:

- when your goals are fairly important but it is also important to preserve your relationship with the other person
- when you and the other person are equally powerful and strongly committed to mutually exclusive goals
- to buy time with temporary settlements (ensuring everybody recognizes that they are temporary)
- to arrive at expedient solutions due to pressure of time
- as the fallback when neither competing nor cooperating is successful for either side

Collaborating[9]

Collaboration is both assertive and cooperative. It involves working with other people to find mutually satisfactory – 'win/win', consensus – agreements.

Collaborating is appropriate:

- when it is essential to find a 'win/win' solution because both sets of interests and concerns are too important to be compromised
- when an agreement will require everybody's commitment to be sustainable, and must therefore be thoroughly 'owned' by everybody
- when a situation is so complex, or so sensitive, that it requires the transformation of relationships as well as agreement on the issues
- when a really good agreement requires people to work together over a period of time

Accommodating

Accommodating is the opposite of competing: cooperative but unassertive. It means neglecting your own interests in your efforts to satisfy those of the other person.

Accommodating is appropriate:

- when it is worth making concessions to demonstrate your reasonableness or generosity
- when the issues are more important to the other person than they are to you, and you have an opportunity to make a goodwill gesture to improve the relationship
- when you are definitely going to lose anyway, and further competition might damage other interests
- when you discover that you are in the wrong, and the advantages of conceding gracefully outweigh the embarrassment involved

---

[9] For an excellent introduction to the collaborative approach see *Everyone Can Win* by Helena Cornelius and Shoshana Faire (Simon & Schuster, 1989)

Avoiding
Avoiding is unassertive and uncooperative: you seek ways to pursue neither your own interests nor those of the other side.

Avoiding is appropriate:
- when an issue is trivial, a symptom of a larger problem, or other matters are more important
- when there is no chance of affecting the situation anyway
- when the potential costs of negotiating outweigh any possible benefits
- when tensions need to be reduced and people need to gain perspective
- when the timing is bad – either the people or the issues are not ready for negotiating

MAKING PROGRESS AS PAINLESS AS POSSIBLE
There are some little things you can do to smooth the path of many negotiations. None of these will resolve the deadlocks, but they can improve the climate and collectively they may make the difference between clinging on to a relationship or watching it go down the tubes.

Agreement will be **harder** if you:	Agreement will be **easier** if you:
Start with *your* solution and insist it is the only one	Start by outlining the issues
Use 'I' statements	Ask 'we' questions
Use 'but . . .'	Use 'and . . .'
Make extravagant demands and ignore others' interests	Explain what you need to achieve and why
Tell people what you want	Ask others what they want
Set deadlines	Explore time constraints for yourself and others
Focus only on the short term	Focus on the short term and the longer term
Ignore relationships	Take appropriate account of relationships
Address issues narrowly and shallowly	Address issues broadly and deeply
Blame the other person for everything	Encourage appropriate and objective allocation of responsibility
Limit the acceptable options for agreement	Widen the options and constantly seek new ones
Focus on differences and polarize the issues	Look for common ground built on areas of agreement
Raise your own expectations and lower those of others	Ensure all expectations are realistic
Conceal and withhold information and resources	Help them to help you

REACHING A MUTUALLY ACCEPTABLE AND REALISTIC AGREEMENT

The final deadlocks are down, agreement is in the bag – and far too many people think this is the end of the negotiation. But it isn't. In fact, if the agreement is at all complex, this is when the problems start, because people often forget that it takes two to tango: you cannot *implement* an agreement unless it works for everybody.

So you have to keep the other people's point of view in mind beyond the negotiation – until, in fact, it has been implemented. This list gives you some criteria which any agreement should meet if it is to be implemented and sustainable. A 'good' agreement:

- is better than anything you or the other person could achieve without negotiating
- satisfies all your shared needs and interests, and preferably some which are not shared
- is the overall best option after consideration of all possible options
- feels legitimate for all those party to it
- is reached efficiently and cost-effectively
- includes commitments which are realistic, practical, and sustainable
- includes a pre-designed safety net in case something goes wrong
- builds trust and invests in a good future working relationship where this is appropriate
- improves communication and understanding and therefore makes the next negotiation easier

If you and your fellow negotiators have negotiated well, you should have no trouble in getting formal agreement: but there are nearly always last-minute snags and hitches as people have 'buyer's remorse' and try to squeeze one last concession. Never leave a negotiation without having something in writing and signed. As a boss of mine used to say: *'In God we trust; everyone else in writing.'*

SKILL DEVELOPMENT

Negotiation is not something you can practise on your own – though I suppose you can practise negotiating with yourself over whether to dig the garden or go to the pub.

You can do quite well, however, by simply becoming more aware of when you are negotiating – childrens' bedtimes, evenings out – and using the checklist below to see how well you have used the opportunity it presents to improve the relationship as well as to achieve an agreement.

Summary

Instead of the usual chapter summary, here is a general checklist to keep with you during any negotiation:

INTERESTS: What do I want? What do they want?

FEARS: What do I/they want to avoid?

VALUES: What is of personal, cultural, religious, symbolic or abstract importance to me/them?

UNCERTAINTIES: What uncertainties are there? How can we reduce them?

OPTIONS: How can we generate more mutually acceptable options?

COMMUNICATION: How can we improve communication and mutual understanding?

RELATIONSHIP: How can we build mutual trust?

REALITIES: What proposals are realistic? Will they work for both sides?

COMMITMENT: How can we demonstrate to each other our commitment to making the agreement sustainable?

7

PROPOSING

> *'There is one thing stronger than all the armies in the world: and that is an idea whose time has come'*
>
> **Victor Hugo**

INTRODUCTION

No, I don't mean getting down on bended knee and making the appropriate speech to your beloved – though, come to think of it, much of what you find in this chapter is as relevant to proposing marriage as to proposing anything else.

We propose all the time. Casually, as in *'Why don't you do the washing-up while I walk the dog'* and formally as in *'We propose a political assembly in which all sections of the community will be represented by direct election of delegates.'* Some proposals are notably more successful than others.

What makes the difference between a successful and unsuccessful proposal? In the last chapter we explored the people skills implicit in negotiation. Had we instead been focusing on the mechanics of negotiation, I would have suggested that one stage in the negotiation process is proposing. How you package and formulate a proposal when negotiating often determines the success or failure of it, and this same principle operates with regard to a proposal in any other context.

Just as you would be unlikely to be successful if your proposal of marriage was inept through poor timing (just after being caught *in flagrante* with your partner's best friend) or sloppy wording (*'Stella – er, I mean Sally – will you . . .'*), so a proposal in any situation has a better chance of being accepted if it follows a few basic principles.[10]

MAKING PROPOSALS

The art of proposing is the art of getting the other person to say '*yes*'. A proposal is made up of two parts:

- *what* you propose

and

- *how* you propose it.

Making a proposal is a bit like making a parachute jump. Once you have walked out of the aeroplane, you cannot get back into it. Likewise, once you have made your proposal, it can be difficult to withdraw it. I always remember one of those old *Doctor* books where the determinedly-bachelor hero, in a drunken stupor, proposes to one of the nurses and wakes up the following morning in horror at what he has done. His friend recognizes the only way out – and suggests he immediately propose to every other nurse in the hospital.

So just as you do not make a parachute jump without careful packing of the parachute and testing of the wind direction, so you do not make a proposal without doing some preparatory work. The preparatory work you do will depend, of course, on the nature of the proposal, but there are some general criteria against which you should measure the quality of any proposal.

Preparing Proposals

A properly prepared proposal should:

- **have a good chance of being accepted and at least not damage your relationship with the other person if rejected.**

You should always try to leave the door open to a new proposal if the first is unacceptable. Providing you:

---

[10] For guidance on proposals across the gender divide, try *Men are From Mars, Women are from Venus* by John Gray (Thorsons, 1993)

- **demonstrate a real appreciation of the other person's needs, interests, concerns – and intelligence**

they will probably be willing to listen to your next attempt. While making a proposal you want to be rejected might sometimes be appropriate as a negotiating ploy (though there may be better ways to achieve the same effect), on the whole you only make proposals to which you want the other person to agree. It may be that you want a simple 'yes', but if you want a more detailed response, or a response which needs a particular condition attached to it (for example, timing):

- **specify the decision you are asking the other person to make.**

Most people are unable to read your mind, and if you really do not want the decision immediately, or you want it made in relation to some other factor, then you must specify it. For example, *'This is my proposal, and I would like you to think it over and give me a decision next week when you have had a chance to talk to the Personnel Department. I need to know whether you will accept this new job, what salary you want, and when you could take it up.'* If you do not do this, you risk your proposal being rejected when it might have been accepted.

Specifying the decision will also help you to prepare a proposal which is

- **potentially and realistically acceptable to the other person's partners, superiors, constituency.**

In other words, it is not enough just to be thinking of the person faced with making the response to your proposal. You also have to think about the people whom they might ask for advice, or whom they will need to convince that what you are proposing is a good idea. If your proposal is not equally designed for them, again it risks being rejected unnecessarily. Sometimes a small tweak to a proposal makes all the difference between acceptance and rejection.

For example, '*I propose that **we** should bid for this contract*' to a colleague may be more likely to elicit a positive response than '*I propose that **you** should bid for this contract*' which could be heard as '*We should go for this providing **you** do all the work*'.

This brings us to the whole matter of how to word a proposal.

Wording Proposals

Think carefully about how you word a proposal and practise it on yourself or a colleague to gauge the effect before you actually say it. Again, the tweaking of the odd word can make the difference between it being accepted and being thrown back in your face.

Here are some basic points to remember:

- **Frame the proposal in the positive: in terms of what you *do* want rather than what you *don't* want.**

This may seem obvious but it is surprising how often I hear people saying something along the lines of '*I propose we should avoid going to the cinema because it will be crowded*'. Saying the cinema is likely to be crowded is fine as part of a discussion about what to do, but it is not helpful as part of a proposal when people will be listening for positive suggestions. Maybe this was why I spent so much of my early adulthood hanging around on pavements in groups of people unable to decide anything.

- **Package the proposal so that it has a number of component parts which can be adjusted or negotiated if necessary.**

It is only after prolonged negotiation that you should offer someone a *take it or leave it* proposal (and only when you do not need them to take it). Leaving some points open to negotiation and possible concession gives the other person an incentive to go on listening; it tells them you are prepared to be flexible, and it also gives you the chance to concede things which do not matter so much to you.

If you are firmly wedded to every part of a proposal, or if it is in one package in which every bit depends on every other, you can end up painting yourself into a corner. It makes you vulnerable to a skilful negotiator.

- **Phrase your proposal in such a way that it sounds as if you are floating an objectively good idea and inviting the other side to join in.**

Try to make your proposal convincing *on its merits* – so it does not look as if you are pushing an idea which is to your benefit alone. Selling an idea on its merits also means it is harder for them to perceive that you are *telling* them what to do.

The word *selling* here is quite appropriate because this is what a good proposal should do – be so well-prepared, crafted and delivered that it sells itself.

RESPONDING TO PROPOSALS

Being on the receiving end of a proposal can be quite as disturbing as having to make one. Here it comes, perhaps out of the blue and delivered by someone who – without the excellent advice provided here – has produced a dog's dinner of a proposal. Bits of it you quite fancy; other bits are ludicrous – and this person wants a reply now, at once, no room for pause or reflection. What do you do?

- Try to respond positively to every proposal.

Even those which are totally ridiculous and an insult to your intelligence? I think 'yes' for the simple reason that while someone is making proposals, even bad proposals, you are still in dialogue with them, and things can always improve. You can usefully ask yourself such pacifying questions as *'How come this person does not understand my point of view? Perhaps I have not explained it clearly?'* And rather than blasting them, you take the opportunity to explain why you cannot accept and your specific reasons for declining. If it is unacceptable without being completely off-beam, rather than simply rejecting it, reply along the lines of *'That it is an interesting idea. Could you expand on it a little?'* It may be that as they discuss it further, you will get a clue about how it might be modified to your mutual advantage.

- Never accept a first proposal, even it if is attractive: if it is their first, it means they have more to offer you.

People never give you everything they can first time around: it is always worth waiting to see what else might be on offer.

- If you have to reject a proposal, explain why by inviting them to see it through your eyes.

How do you reject a proposal gracefully? Basically, by getting them to feel that if they were in your shoes, they would also reject it. But don't stop there. If you are still interested in them making a proposal which would be acceptable.

- When you reject a proposal, tell them what *specifically* would have to be changed in order for it to become acceptable.

So as well as not accepting the first proposal, don't reject it out of hand either, in case you lose what might be good in it. In fact, maintain momentum and optimism for as long as you can:

- Respond to proposals in a manner and tone which indicate that you believe agreement is possible, and that it is just a matter of finding the right package.

If the other person is doing the proposing, you may be in the position of them needing you more than you need them. This may be your good fortune, but be aware that dependency breeds resentment.

OBSTACLES TO PROPOSALS – AND HOW TO OVERCOME THEM

You keep making proposals to someone – and you have done your homework so they are proposals which are eminently sensible and should be acceptable – but somehow you never get to that magic 'yes'.

Here are some common *procedural* reasons – i.e. reasons to do with *how* they are presented rather than *what* they are – why proposals may not be accepted even when they should be.

Common Obstacles

- **Differences of culture or values**

It may be that you have overlooked some underlying differences between you and the other person. Could it be, for example, that you are dealing with a woman who does not like the fact that it is a man doing the proposing? Or vice versa? Explore any differences you may discern.

- **Emotional barriers**

Perhaps there is some past event coming between your proposal and its acceptance. Create a safe moment (*'OK, let's go off the record a minute . . .'*) and ask *'What prevents you accepting my proposal?'*

- **Apparent inflexibility**

Ask the other person to clarify their needs and interests, ask in what way they are not being met, or describe the logjam objectively and ask for their suggestions on what to do next. It may also be useful to ask for a longer-term vision of what they are trying to achieve, and the consequences for that vision of their not accepting your proposal.

- **Personality clash**

You could try acknowledging the problem and suggest some ground rules to prevent it getting in the way, or suggest meeting the other person informally to explore what exactly is going wrong.

• Issues too daunting

Sometimes people cannot respond positively to a proposal because they find the whole subject too terrifying: they do not want responsibility for making such an important decision. In this case, see if you can reduce your proposal to its component parts, making it more digestible.

• Too much uncertainty

Making decisions in response to proposals presumes the existence of the information on which you need to base a decision. Sometimes that information is missing, or the person is embarrassed to admit that there is too much uncertainty for them to make a firm decision. Once you know this is the problem, you can perhaps tackle it jointly, seeking further information, guidance, or expert advice.

• Unrealistic expectations

Another common reason for a proposal being rejected is that it does not measure up to the other person's expectations — and again embarrassment may prevent them admitting it. If you suspect this may be the case, try to discover what they did expect, and gently explore how realistic that expectation was.

It may also be that they have passed on unrealistic expectations to others, and therefore feel unable to compromise. One way out of this is to review their priorities with them, and hope that your more realistic proposal may be seen in a wider context, or in relation to other factors.

• Loss of momentum

If all the momentum seems to be seeping out of your dialogue, try listing proposals which have already been accepted, and reviewing the pressures and constraints on both of you.

SKILL DEVELOPMENT

So there is more to making proposals than meets the eye?
Try the following exercise with another person and see how you do:

Person A: describes a situation in which **Person B** would
have to make a proposal.
For example:

- a teenage child wants to borrow the car to go to a late-
  night party;
- it's your honeymoon and the hotel wants to give you
  a room with two single beds rather than a double;
- your neighbour wants to build a ten-foot fence
  between your gardens;
- your partner wants to work part-time rather than full-
  time.

Person B: makes a proposal to resolve any differences.

After each proposal, discuss
- how likely it would be to be accepted and
- how it could be improved to make it more acceptable.

Then swap roles and try another situation.

Summary

Effective proposals:
- have a good chance of being accepted
- demonstrate concern for the other person's needs,
  interests, concerns and intelligence
- specify the decision you are asking the other person to
  make
- are potentially and realistically acceptable to the other
  person's partners, superiors, constituency
- are framed in the positive
- are packaged to have a number of component parts
  which can be adjusted or negotiated.
- are phrased in such a way that it sounds as if you are
  floating a good idea and inviting them to join in.

8

COUNSELLING

'The diseases of the mind are more destructive than those of the body'

Marcus Tullius Cicero

INTRODUCTION

Some people think there is too much counselling around today. They see counsellors rushed to the sites of accidents or violent incidents; they see people receiving money in compensation for Post Traumatic Stress Disorder; they feel the good old tradition of the stiff upper lip is being eroded by the wimpishness of the junior generations. *'We never needed counselling in the war,'* they say, *'so why should you lot need so much of it for these smaller traumas?'*

Why indeed? This is a useful starting point for a chapter on counselling, because you may be wondering why it is even included here – other than to obey the dictates of fashion. Counselling is obviously a 'people skill', but surely it deserves a whole book, rather than cursory inclusion among other skills? I am including it because I think the ability to offer counselling to others is actually a pretty basic skill. Also, because I have so often heard people saying something along the lines of *'So-and-so came to cry on my shoulder and I really did not know where to start.'*

Another reason is today's newspaper.[11] It quotes the following, terrifying statistics: from 1984–94 there was a 70 per cent rise in suicides among boys and young men aged 13–24. Nineteen-thousand people attempt suicide every year. There are 44,000 hospital admissions every year for self-harm among under-25s. In the last thirty years the incidence

---

[11] *The Independent*, 17 July 1996

of depression among children and young adults has increased enormously, although depression in the general population has not changed. The reasons for this increase are hotly debated: it seems that family breakdown and the general pressures of contemporary life have much to answer for.

I think these are all good reasons why every adult should have at least some basic knowledge of counselling. We should be able to offer emotional first aid in the same way as we should know how to give artificial respiration and stick plasters on the walking wounded.

The aim of this chapter is to help you know where to start, but certainly not where to end. It will not turn you into anything approaching a professional counsellor, but it may help you to know when someone needs a professional rather than a friend, and it may help you respond to the friend who does indeed just need a shoulder to dampen.

WHAT IS COUNSELLING?

Let's begin by understanding that 'counselling' can range from offering that famous shoulder to someone who needs a brief moan to several years with a professionally trained and qualified therapist. My spin here is towards the first: I am thinking of the person who, at home, or at work, finds themselves with a colleague or a friend in distress, and needs to respond sensitively and sensibly until either the crisis is over, or the person is passed on to an appropriate professional.

So, please note any professional counsellors or therapists who happen upon this book – I am not suggesting group therapy in the coffee break or Jungian dream-analysis over lunch. Yet even very basic counselling needs to rest on some understanding of what such a time with another person demands. Here are what I regard as the fundamentals of counselling:

Relationship: Counselling always involves a relationship which has to be qualitatively different from our everyday relationships if it is to be of value. In particular, it has to rest on warmth, sincerity, and genuine regard.

Skills: Even elementary counselling depends on skills such as listening and empathizing.

Self-help: Counselling is sometimes misunderstood as telling other people what to do. It is in fact about helping the other person to make their own choices – it is the counsellor's job to help them get into a position to be able to do that.

Equality: There is a huge temptation to see the person being counselled as in some way inferior to the person doing the counselling. I think counselling only works when there is mutual respect and affirmation of equal worth.

Purpose: The sort of counselling we are interested in here needs to have some definite purpose, direction, and an idea of what it is intended to achieve. There needs to be some difference between counselling and a good chat – which is not to say that a good chat is not sometimes more appropriate than actual counselling.

HOW YOU MIGHT USE COUNSELLING

In what circumstances might it be appropriate for you – as friend or colleague – to get into a counselling role with someone?

Problem-solving

Many times people will seek help from you because they have a specific problem. Your first task will be to discover, with them, whether this is a 'presenting problem'. For example, someone may come to you worried about their workload. As you talk about it, you discover that the real problem is that they are drinking too much and their marriage is going wrong. Overwork is the presenting problem: the problem which gives them the reason – or excuse, if you like – to seek help.

Decision-making

A friend comes to you for help because they have two job offers, and which they choose could make a vital difference to the direction of their career. This sort of counselling involves helping people to make a limited number of specific decisions. Your job will be to help them assess each job on its merits and in relation to their wider life and career intentions.

Emotional Healing

People who are emotionally injured often suppress – for years and whole lifetimes – the real impact of that injury. As more such cases come to light and are publicized – for example, until a few years ago the physical and emotional abuse of children was not much discussed publicly – so more people feel able to discuss their own experiences.

If someone comes to you to talk about the scars of their childhood, and is clearly deeply distressed, then offer them immediate love and support, and as part of that encourage them to go for professional help.

Crisis Management

Your colleague turns up one morning and tells you her son is on drugs, her husband has run off with a barman, the car is being repossessed, the cat has been run over, and the washing machine has flooded the house.

Crisis management counselling is about helping people whose ability to cope has run out because they are simply overwhelmed by the weight, number or complexity of the challenges they face. Your job in such a situation, apart from offering friendship and support, might be to help them separate things and deal with one at a time. You may find that they are responding to the convergence of events, and that not all of them have actually happened that morning as they set off for work.

What they need from you is some anchorage: a rock they can tie themselves to as the tides rush around them. You may find that ringing a plumber and finding out about local drug projects is as valuable as any counselling as such.

General Support

There does not have to be a crisis before you offer to help. This is the thinking behind the 'Employee Assistance Programmes' which are run by some enlightened employers. Although these are relatively new, there is some anecdotal evidence that they can help organizations to reduce problems such as absenteeism and staff turnover. The programmes offer confidential counselling to employees for problems such as alcoholism, marital strife, stress and so on. The fact that the programme is available may be as important as how much it is actually used.

Training and Mentoring

Not all counselling looks like counselling. I find as a trainer that I do quite a lot of informal counselling in the evenings and during breaks. Training is about developing people, and helping to uncover and dissolve the blocks which limit their progress. Good training often reveals to people feelings of which they were not previously aware, and it is natural that they should turn to the person who stimulated them.

Mentoring is similar. It involves the establishment of a relationship between an older and a younger person. The idea is that the older person gives the younger person the benefit of their experience, and holds their hand as they climb the ladder.

MANAGING COUNSELLING

I think it is useful to be aware of the dilemmas which face anybody who finds themselves in the role of counsellor. Remember, this relationship with someone is different from the relationship you would have with the same person in a different context. The friend or colleague who exposes their vulnerabilities to you is seeking something different from your normal relationship. They may not know what this something is, and neither may you: but it will be there, and it inevitably affects how you conduct this relationship.

Let's look at some of the basic choices both you and the other person face:

You:	*Friend/colleague/other person:*
Can I help you?	Can she/he help?
Should I help?	Is this the right person to talk to?
What do I say?	What do I want to hear?
How deep do I go?	How much do I want to reveal?
Can I cope with this?	How much can I lay on him/her?
Do I want to do this again?	Do I trust him/her?

These are the thoughts and questions which will probably be swirling around in both people's heads, and associated with them will be feelings ranging from *'I really don't want to get into this'* to *'Help! What on earth am I doing telling this person things about me I have never told anyone'*.

These kinds of thoughts can best be handled by having

some predetermined sense of how happy – if at all – you are to be in the position of counselling someone, and – assuming you are happy to take on this role – how to manage it. The problem with trying to 'manage' counselling is that it can remove the spontaneity which gives genuine warmth to any relationship, just as putting into practice good listening skills can make your listening seem stilted and unnatural until you get the hang of them.

Offering any framework for managing a counselling relationship also courts the dangers implicit in any 'amateur' counselling: it may give you more confidence than you should have. Is it more dangerous to offer nothing at all, or to offer something? I am plumping for the latter and hoping you appreciate that no packaged process is a substitute for in-depth training.

I have adapted the following framework from the model offered by Richard Nelson-Jones in his excellent *Practical Counselling and Helping Skills*[12], which I would thoroughly recommend to anyone interested in this field, both because it will alert you to the complexities involved in counselling, and because it is the only book I know in this rather solemn field which includes some great jokes.

Nelson-Jones offers what he calls the DOSIE model:

D – **Describe** and identify problem(s)
O – **Operationalize** the problem(s)
S – **Set goals** and negotiate interventions
I – **Intervene**
E – **Exit**

Nelson-Jones is writing for a professional audience, however, and I do not intend to reproduce his model in full.

---

[12] *Practical Counselling and Helping Skills* by Richard Nelson-Jones (last edition Tassel Educational 1988, ISBN 0-304-31469-2)

Here is an outline of it, setting out his five stages and indicating something of what might happen in each. For the sake of brevity I am using the word 'client' to describe the person you are helping.

Stage 1: Describe and identify problem(s)

You have to begin by building an alliance with the client: telling them both verbally and through manner and tone that you are on their side. This does not mean that you will agree with everything they do: condoning poor behaviour or colluding with deceit or dishonesty helps nobody – least of all the client. But in order to challenge them effectively when necessary, they need to know that you have their best interests at heart.

With the alliance in place, you can work on describing and defining the problems they face. Through listening, questioning and empathizing, you will begin to help them make sense of the chaos, and put their situation into some kind of structure and perspective. Sometimes this is the single most useful thing a counselling friend can do.

Stage 2: Operationalize

Operationalizing means getting to grips with the details. Discovering, for example, who is really responsible for what; what specifically needs to happen; what skills the client will need in order to resolve particular issues.

It is also the stage at which the client, beginning to see some hope of getting out of their hole, may begin to appreciate different perceptions of their situation. No solutions have been reached yet, but they may be gaining new insights and beginning to acknowledge what solutions will require of them. Your job is to encourage and facilitate this process, and work with them to discover the strength to continue.

Stage 3: Set goals and negotiate interventions

At this stage you can begin to define with them what the

outcome of the process should be. One of the things I was never taught, when I first did a counselling course, is that it is very difficult to get anywhere if you don't know where you are going. Helping the client to describe their goals, perhaps in some detail, gives you both a firm sense of direction, and also some idea where you are in relation to them.

So if your client's goal is 'to feel happy', you would want to ask what 'feeling happy' means to them. *'How will you know when you are happy?'* might be a useful starting point. If their definition of happiness is having fur coats and a large yacht, well, at least you know where you are.

This is also the time to clarify the client's expectations of you. If you are just a friend and a colleague, this is your moment to point it out, explain the limits of what you can do, perhaps the constraints on your time. Failure to do so can cause problems later. (*'When I turned to you for help, you soon got bored and said you couldn't.'*)

Stage 4: Intervene
By now you can begin to build upwards from the foundations you have laid. You can work on particular areas: pointing out, for example, when a person is giving themselves negative messages; setting 'homework' for them to do: *'Every time you find yourself thinking that you cannot do something, I want you to note it down, pause, and tell yourself how you are going to do it. Bring your notes to our next meeting and we will go through them.'*

We are in danger of straying into the territory of the professional counsellor from here on, but this may be useful if someone is frightened about what going to counselling might entail.

The intervening stage is also about increasing the client's skills – identifying where they are betrayed by gaps in their capabilities. All help of this kind must ultimately turn into self-help: you cannot do more for the person than they can learn to do for themselves. Your role is facilitator and friend, not permanent scaffolding.

Stage 5: Exit

Before you leave, consolidate the work you have done. Review the new skills and perceptions, anticipate what may be around the corner, help the person to get along without you. Saying goodbye can be one of the trickiest points of all, but it is also a measure of how successful you have been.

Look after yourself

It is no coincidence that people in the helping professions have high suicide rates. Helping is usually messy. It does not proceed in neat stages. You seem to make progress and then you are back at square one. It is also unrealistic to think that you can remain perfectly detached, the facilitator of someone else's life. It puts a strain on you. It puts a strain on your other, normal relationships.

All these are additional arguments for persuading severely distressed people to get professional help if they need it. Do not take on more than your own life can manage.

SKILL DEVELOPMENT

Find a professionally run course by a reputable body such as the British Association for Counselling.

Summary

Counselling is a smart word for helping.

Helping other people deal with their emotional hurts is as basic a people skill as being able to bandage a wound.

If someone comes to you for help:

- Listen
- Empathize

- Ask questions to help them be clear about what they want
- Offer support and friendship
- Encourage self-help
- If their problems are serious, encourage them to seek professional help.

9

CONFRONTING

INTRODUCTION

Lurking in the background throughout this book has been
the matter of 'difficult people'. Confronting them is what
you do when every other skill has failed, or when the
nature of the person or the situation does not allow the slow
cultivation of an influential relationship based on mutual
trust and understanding.

Most books giving you the benefit of the author's wisdom
on 'how to confront difficult people' tend to take one of
two approaches. They divide people into types, and specify
ways of dealing with each type. This is fine, except that
there is the danger of specifying so many types that you will
be so busy trying to decide what type a particular person fits
into that you will altogether forget what else you should be
doing with them.

The other common approach is what is known as 'behaviour modification'. To me it always sounds like something
dreamed up by one of the James Bond villains intent on rul-
ing the world. Behaviour modification basically means
changing the stimuli to which an individual is exposed so as
to bring about a desired behavioural response. In English,
that means giving your kid a lollipop every time it does
what you want – a blend of bribery, appeasement and
manipulation.

I want to suggest something different: simpler in approach,
harder to make work, but I think both more ethical and

ultimately more satisfying when it does. It starts from the idea that dealing with difficult people – remembering that you are also a difficult person for some people – has to be about encouraging them to *change*. This is asking for trouble because people are always telling me that other people do not change. They nod wisely into their beer and say lugubriously, and depressingly, *'The trouble is you can't change the way people behave. That's human nature.'*

As time goes on I become increasingly unsure what people mean by 'human nature', other than an excuse for every human failing. Of course you can change how people behave. Why else would we spend so much time and money on education, and training, and psychologists, and management development courses, and appraisal schemes? And why else would the bookshops of the world be groaning under the weight of books about how people can help themselves to change?

Human beings are extraordinarily adaptable. And to those of you who are thinking to yourselves *'Yes, but it takes time . . .'*, I would say that you have swallowed the self-interested propaganda from the 'therapy' profession which insists that only several years on the couch can make much difference. To be fair, even the therapists are recognizing that human beings can change pretty fast when they want to: how else could we have people falling in love 'at first sight', or doing something 'quite out of character' because the situation demands it. People change very fast indeed *providing they are motivated to do so.*

This is the first part of the secret of dealing with the people you find difficult, and it springs from a certain attitude towards them. So the first part of this chapter looks at what kind of attitude it is useful to have when you confront, or are confronted by, someone you find difficult.

GET YOUR BASIC ATTITUDES RIGHT

Take these to heart:

1. **There are no 'difficult people' as such**, but there are limits to our ability to deal with certain individuals. Certain difficult individuals may resemble certain other difficult individuals but, like the rest of us, they are individuals first, second and third.

2. **There are no irrational people**, but there are limits to our ability and our desire to understand those who think differently from us. People always act rationally – *from their point of view*. The further that view is from ours, the harder it is for us to understand their reasoning.

3. **People always do the best they can** – with the personal resources (from their upbringing, education, experience etc.) they have, and within the constraints their map of the world imposes on them. To change what they do, you may have to help them develop new or different resources, or a new map and understanding of the world.

4. **Our primary tool is our own behaviour** – the more flexible we are, the more likely we are to find a way to influence them. If what we do does not work, we have to be prepared to do something different, and go on trying different approaches, until we find one that works.

5. **Before we can influence someone we have to:**
   - invest time and effort in listening so that we
   - gain some insight into *why* they are doing what they are doing and
   - understand how our behaviour affects their behaviour and then we need to
   - decide what *specifically* we want them to do differently.

6. We need to accept that people change their behaviour when they have a good enough reason to change it, and when it feels safe enough to do so.

The real challenge is to discover what, for each individual, from moment to moment, is *good enough* and *safe enough*.

These six points I deliver regularly in workshops and training sessions. The responses range from acceptance to outrage. The two most common questions are: *'Are they true?'*, to which I respond, *'I don't know: but it is useful to believe they are . . .'*; and *'Why the hell should I change my behaviour when it is theirs which is the problem?'*, to which I respond, *'You should only choose to change your behaviour if you want what you can achieve by changing it more than what you have to give up by doing so.'*

BE FLEXIBLE IN YOUR OWN BEHAVIOUR

People behave with a mixture of calculation and spontaneity. This is part of the reason why it is difficult to prescribe behaviour in any single situation or in dealing with any particular individual. In the real world it is impossible to say that getting furious and yelling at someone is always wrong. The books may tells us that 'threatening' behaviour is wrong, but experience tells us that sometimes a hefty if metaphorical boot up the backside can be therapeutic for both booter and bootee.

This makes it very difficult to offer cogent advice on what to do about someone who is being 'difficult': so much depends on the individual concerned, the circumstances, and what you are trying to achieve. This is what makes attitude number five on p.93 so important. Here it is again:

Before we can influence someone we have to:

- invest time and effort in listening so that we

- gain some insight into *why* they are doing what they are doing and
- understand how our behaviour affects their behaviour and then we need to
- decide what *specifically* we want them to do differently.

Once we know these things, we can begin to think about changing our behaviour in such a way that it will influence the other person's. There will be cries of 'manipulation' about this if I do not explain further.

Manipulative behaviour is, by dictionary definition, 'unfair': it is behaviour which denies the manipulated person a choice. Much manipulative behaviour is in fact calculated but unconscious, like the child who whines for a sweet from the check-out counter while a harassed parent struggles to pack the shopping. I am not proposing that you should behave in such a way that another person feels coerced into doing what you want. I am proposing that you should behave in a way that enables the other person to respond differently to you should they care to do so.

You will notice that I am carefully still trying to avoid describing types of people but instead talking about behaviour. This brings me to a principle which is my crossover point from attitudes to strategies:

People are more than their behaviour.

Please understand that however difficult it may be, you must try to separate the individual from the behaviour we find difficult. This principle is fundamental to a civilized approach to other people: *hate the sin, love the sinner.*

PATTERNS OF BEHAVIOUR

I want to outline four particular patterns of behaviour which people often find difficult, and suggest how we can respond to each. These four patterns of behaviour are not, of course, the only ones you will encounter, but they serve as a useful starting point for learning to respond in different ways to different behaviours (and I find most people cannot easily remember more than four anyway). These are also the four patterns of behaviour about which I hear most complaints and requests for help.

Remember two things:
- that the tactics suggested here are designed to complement those basic attitudes described earlier: use these tactics without those attitudes, and they may be worse than useless
- 'confronting' does not mean behaving aggressively: it means tackling the problem rather than ducking it.

1. Bullying

Behaviour:
Domineering, insensitive to others, determined to control, compete and win at all costs.

Intention of confrontation:
- To turn competing and controlling into collaboration and co-operation
- To teach them new ways of achieving what they want

Tactics:	**Your behaviour:**
1. Get their respect	• Stand up to them and make it clear that you will not be pushed around.
	• Look them in the eye
2. Get their attention	• Address them formally, and use their name frequently and firmly.
	• Do not let them interrupt you or shout you down. If they do, listen, and then repeat what you

were going to say.

3. Clarify what they want	• Ask particularly about their bottom line, and for details and specifics. • Summarize back to them. • Speak in a crisp, clear, firm 'no-nonsense' voice.
4. Say what you want	• Tell them your needs and interests and why they are important to you. • Be positive and assume success.
5. Make a proposal	• Tell them what you propose and why it will get you both what you want. • Speak calmly and confidently. • It may help to number your points when you speak. • Ask if they have any questions.
6. Make commitments	• Summarize: tell them what you will do by when and how you will do it – if necessary in writing.

2. Inflexibility

Behaviour:
Unwillingness to listen to new ideas; minds rigid and closed, sometimes obsessively focused on details and on the past; inclined to hold grudges.

Intention of confrontation
• To get the person on your side
• To unblock them to the possibility of other perceptions

Tactics:	**Your behaviour:**
1. Get their story	• Listen, listen, listen: be prepared to go over the situation time and again, paraphrasing their precise words.
	• Take lots of notes, acknowledge everything they say.
	• Ask questions so that they can demonstrate their splendid knowledge.
	• Discover where they are correct, and where their prejudices are distorting their judgment.
	• Avoid direct challenges to them.
2. Build momentum and relationship	• Slowly and steadily build a shared description of the situation.
	• Make them aware of your own expertise, but without contradicting them; avoid *'but'* – use *'and'*.
	• Give them a role as your expert: form a problem–solving alliance.
3. Get them to identify options for change	• Ask for their opinions about possible ways forward.
	• Get them to set out advantages and disadvantages of each option; ask *what if* questions.
	• If you have a preferred option, introduce it as a hypothetical solution on which you would value their advice.
4. Get them to specify commitments	• Ask for specific details about how an option would work in practice.

- Ask how they could contribute to a specific outcome.
- Make sure they have 'ownership' of any solution.

5. Emphasize evaluation
- Ask for written reports, data, evidence and follow-up.
- Identify a continuing role for them.

3. Posturing

Behaviour:
Attention-seeking, pretentious, affected, showing-off, self-indulgent, egotistical.

Intention of confrontation:
- To give them clear boundaries for their behaviour
- To make them more aware of others' needs

Tactics:	Your behaviour:
1. Indulge them	<ul><li>Give them the opportunity to show off, strut their stuff.</li><li>Respond with faintly amused tolerance, but no applause or encouragement.</li></ul>
2. Set boundaries	<ul><li>Focus their attention on a specific issue.</li><li>Give plenty of time to talk, bringing them back to the issue any time they deviate towards themselves.</li></ul>
3. Maintain boundaries	<ul><li>Ask detailed questions about needs of others.</li><li>Respond positively to serious, non self-centred behaviour;</li></ul>

negatively to self-indulgent behaviour.

4. Get commitments	● Insist on commitments which reflect new boundaries and awareness of others' needs.
	● Set time-frame.
	● Emphasize rewards and credits, and consequences of failure.
5. Follow up	● Check details of actions.
	● Be generous about their achievements.
	● Be specific about their short-comings.

4. Passivity

Behaviour:
Apparently directionless, sudden flashes of passive aggression such as sarcasm or emotional manipulation; unwillingness to make commitments, sometimes a reluctance even to respond.

Intention of confrontation
● To clarify actual needs and interests
● To get realistic commitments

Tactics:	**Your behaviour:**
1. Demonstrate empathy	● Ask empathetic questions.
	● Use a soft, low voice, speak slowly, make the situation safe.
2. Discover reasons for passivity	● Identify internal conflicts.
	● Ask about obstacles to progress.
	● Use 'we' and 'us'; build a relationship.
	● Be generous and specific about

their achievements; build confidence.

3. Reduce obstacles	• Listen carefully to all their concerns.
	• Identify and isolate specific problems, break down all obstacles to component parts and bited-sized chunks.
	• Always sandwich any necessary criticism between praise.
	• Emphasize support structures and safety nets.
4. Specify decisions	• Work with them to identify options and advantages and disadvantages of each.
	• Specify consequences of decisions.
	• Discuss explicit time-frames.
5. Get commitments	• Break commitments into component parts.
	• Emphasize team and joint actions.
	• Specify timing and actions involved in each commitment.
	• Offer support throughout.

GOING FORWARD[13]

There is always a reason for people behaving as they do. Passive behaviour, for example, is often the result of people's internal divisions: they cannot decide what to do, so they opt to do nothing. Passive behaviour is an extreme reaction to something most of us experience. Few of us are

---

[13] For a wholly progressive approach to conflict in general, see *The Magic of Conflict* by Thomas Crum (Touchstone 1987)

'single-minded' about what we want to achieve: *'Part of me wants to do* this; *part of me wants to do* that'. This reflects the school of thought which says that all conflict is the external projection of internal conflict.

People's behaviour is never 'mindless' or 'irrational' and it is never helpful to label it as such. You sometimes hear about someone being 'irrationally angry,' for example. A little understanding of anger reveals how ignorant this is. We flip into anger because it is easier, less complicated, than admitting to ourselves, let alone to others, our confusions, frustrations, insecurities. Anger is nearly always a substitute emotion as well as the expression of honest rage: it is a symptom of other feelings. When someone gets angry, take time to listen and discover the real sources of their anger.

Let me repeat – people are more than their behaviour. Remember that, and you will not want to stick them in boxes, or write them off as hopeless and irrational. Other people are a challenge; the more difficult you find them the greater the challenge they are. Regard every person as an opportunity to learn more about the infinite variety of the species, and you may even begin to enjoy your difficult people.

SKILL DEVELOPMENT
The key to using your own behaviour to influence that of others is flexibility: if what you are doing is not working, do something different and go on doing something different until you find an approach which works.

Exercise
Try this as an exercise with two other people using these four tactics as a starter, for about ten minutes:

Person A: role-plays one of the four patterns of behaviour around a specific issue.

Person B: identifies behaviour and uses the appropriate tactics.

Person C: observes.

At the end of the ten minutes, discuss effectiveness of tactics and how they could be improved for responding to that
behaviour in that situation.

Summary
1. There are no difficult people . . .
- just limits to our patience
- and our people skills

2. There are no irrational people . . .
- just limits to our understanding

3. People do the best they can
- with the resources they have
- with their map of the world

4. To change the way others behave we use our own
   behaviour to
- make them feel safe
- and resourceful
- give them a good enough reason to change

5. We have to know what we want them to do –
- specifically

6. We have to be flexible –
- if what we are doing is not working . . . we have to do
  something different

10

PREVENTING

> *'There are a thousand hacking at the branches of evil to one who is striking at its root'*
>
> **Henry David Thoreau**

INTRODUCTION

Prevention is better than cure. Or is it? Sometimes an out-right battle between people is the only way to clear the air. By 'preventing', though, I mean making sure that any conflict between people − if it has to happen − is prevented from becoming destructive. If you have to have air-clearing battles, let's make sure they do the job: let's get at the roots.

But are they really necessary? If you can prevent the risks of destructive interpersonal showdowns, while at the same time reaping the rewards of creative tension between people, then surely that is to be preferred. It is certainly something you might want to debate before implementing any of the ideas in this chapter: if your organization depends on periodic blood on the carpet, skip the next pages. Or be prepared for some proactive conflict prevention.

PREVENTING PEOPLE PROBLEMS

In a sense, all of the ideas in this book are about preventing people problems, but this chapter is aimed primarily at people in organizations, though there is no reason why the same ideas could not, with a little ingenuity, be applied to a home or a marriage or a partnership.

It starts from the assumption of an organization which experiences conflict on a regular basis, and takes you stage-by-stage through a process for channelling it and making it more constructive. The ideas here have been developed by that small and heroic band of people in the Alternative

Dispute Resolution (ADR) movement, who are trying to encourage people to use less hostile and adversarial methods to resolve all kinds of disputes. These ideas have been influenced by one particular book, *Getting Disputes Resolved*[14], which introduces the idea of designing dispute resolution and conflict prevention systems into the way organizations work. The following brief description of what seems to work is based largely on this book.

DISPUTE PREVENTION AND RESOLUTION SYSTEMS

The basic idea of a dispute prevention system is that high-cost methods of dispute resolution, such as arbitration and litigation, are replaced whenever possible by lower-cost methods, such as negotiation and mediation. If negotiation does not work, that is the time to bring in a mediator; if mediation also fails, then you try a simplified form of arbitration; if those involved will not agree to that, only then do you start using more complex and expensive measures. The skill comes in designing how the system operates in a specific situation.

The two immediately most useful applications of this systematic approach to endemic conflict are within internally divided organizations, and between organizations and their regular clients or customers. A dispute resolution system is therefore a useful – one might say essential – tool for organizations working towards a 'total quality' commitment, or to improving customer services. Both are dependent to a large extent upon the quality of the relationships among staff. Poor customer care is almost invariably an indication of poor management and poor relationships within the organization. This relationship between internal change and external achievement is not always as clearly recognized as it might be.

---

[14] *Getting Disputes Resolved: Designing Systems to Cut the Costs of Conflict* by William Ury, Jeanne Brett and Stephen Goldberg (Jossey-Bass, 1989)

When to Consider a Dispute Resolution System

The impetus for the design and implementation of a dispute resolution system is usually the result of one or more of the following situations:

- A crisis within the existing dispute resolution system (for example, internal tribunals or disciplinary hearings) reveals that it is too costly, too slow, too cumbersome, or people lack confidence in its fairness or effectiveness.
- Many broadly similar disputes are occurring and being dealt with on a piecemeal and therefore expensive basis.
- The nature, volume or intensity of disputes is imposing unacceptable strains on other parts of the organization.
- The organization is in a period of change which involves new relationships and partnerships with considerable benefits for all concerned, but because of this also a heightened risk of disputes.

Note that 'organization ' includes any regular pattern of repeat relationships, as well as any type of organization. Dispute resolution systems have been implemented in bodies ranging from massive corporations to schools and hospitals.

How to implement a dispute resolution system

Stage 1: Research the Existing System – or Lack of It

Most organizations do not respond systematically to conflict because they do not know with enough precision what disputes are occurring and how they are being managed and resolved. Before any significant work can be done to improve dispute handling and prevent people-problems it is essential to do a conflict audit:

- What kinds of disputes are involved

- How many there are
- Are there particular trigger points or warning signs?
- Who gets involved in these disputes?
- What the current cost is
- What processes are currently being used to resolve disputes
- If there are existing mechanisms through which disputes are supposed to be handled – for example, complaints or grievance procedures, staff or partnership meetings – are they being used? If not, why are they not functioning properly?
- What is happening when people try to resolve disputes? What are the obstacles to successful negotiation? What happens when negotiations break down?
- Why are some procedures used more than others? How satisfactory are such procedures – and from whose point of view?
- What are the costs of existing procedures? What effect do the various procedures have on present and future relationships?
- How often do the same disputes recur because they are never properly resolved?

The research necessary to gather this information will in itself be quite valuable, and not just for what you learn. People are generally quite wary of talking about conflict. It is a bit like death or body odour: it happens to all of us but we prefer not to dwell on it. Merely sitting people down and discovering who fights with whom, about what, and the impact of this on those around them, and on the organization as a whole, can be therapeutic.

The word 'therapeutic' is deliberate. It is useful to understand conflict as a kind of illness. It is not always bad (nothing like a dose of flu to catch up on your reading) but it always carries certain costs (the file pile when you get back to work). Conflict, like illness, always happens for a reason, and sometimes it is a vehicle for changing a lot more than just its immediate causes. Just as the person who survives a heart attack may resolve to spend more time with their children, so an organization faced with its internal conflicts may put more emphasis on customer care (because poor customer care is one regular result of internal conflict).

Stage 2: Consult with Potential Users of a Dispute Resolution System (DRS)

As a successful DRS depends heavily on the commitment of those who will use it to make it work, it is essential that they are fully consulted about both its design and implementation. The people consulted should include at least the following:

- All who will be affected by the new system within the organization
- All outside the organization who may be involved in it at some time, notably business partners, customers and potential parties to disputes
- Any potential third parties, ombudsmen, or regulators
- Any consumer organizations, lobby groups, or shareholder groups

The consultation stage is important not only because it supplements the research stage and provides essential intelligence to inform the design stage, but because it will indicate the degree and speed of cultural change required for the workforce to accept the new system, and the likely training requirements.

Most people respond to conflict with the traditional *fight* or *flight* impulse: that last hangover from our Stone Age inheritance. For all the millions of years since, though, you might think there is a sabre-tooth tiger around the corner when it comes to talking about conflict, because many people, in my experience, find it hard even to conceive of other responses. The ADR movement is working on it.

Stage 3: Design the System

The design of new systems for managing disputes is based on the information gained from the conflict audit, and builds on the strengths while eliminating the weaknesses of existing procedures. There are six basic principles in designing a dispute resolution system:

1. Dispute procedures need to be arranged in a low-to-high cost sequence.

2. Preventing disputes almost always costs less than either winning or resolving them; suppression or appeasement can end up costing more.

3. The most cost-effective of all dispute resolution systems is problem-solving negotiation between those directly concerned at the point of first impact.

4. Each procedure should be exhausted before the next is introduced, and each should allow return to the previous procedure if appropriate.

5. There should be consultation before, monitoring during, and feedback after each use of the system.

6. New systems need motivation, leadership, skills and resources to make them work.

Most dispute resolution systems utilize staged processes of intervention going from the least interventionist to the most interventionist. The least interventionist, direct negotiation at the point of dispute, is also the most informal, and allows the disputants most control over the outcome. The most interventionist, referral to an outside tribunal, arbitrator or judge, is the most expensive, most risky for those who do it, and most damaging to relationships within the organization. The ultimate achievement of every dispute

resolution system is to prevent disputes ever happening –
because people   have learned to anticipate and deal with
their causes.

It is usual that different types of dispute require different
degrees of intervention, and different 'entry points' to the
system. The final design must ensure the system is 'user-
friendly', easily comprehended both inside and outside the
organization, and that the entry points are well publicized
and easily available.

The word 'design' is not used lightly. You literally have to
design every detail of every stage of the process, taking into
account everything from the type of organization and its
culture, possibly even to the characters of individual depart-
ments or sites.

So, if Bloggs Containers regularly loses work days because
the supervisor cannot stand the site manager, both those
people need to know how to use the dispute resolution
system, and must feel neither intimidated by it nor embarrassed to confess their need for it. It might be appropriate
for the service to be advertised prominently on a notice-
board, in a company news sheet, or in regular meetings
between management and staff.

Stage 4: Implementation and Evaluation
All who will be affected by the new system must be edu-
cated about it. As with any innovation, the commitment of
senior management is essential, as is the education of all staff
in contact with potential users. If you are setting up a system
to respond to conflict with people outside the organization,
the training of telephonists is particularly important, especially for systems designed to deal with public complaints.

Adequate records and statistics need to be kept for short and
long-term evaluation of the system's response to its objectives. The evaluation needs to survey all involved, from

disputants and their representatives to interveners, trainers and system supporters. While the immediate cost savings on specific disputes are useful indicators of success, it is important that the overall impact of the system on the organization should also be monitored.

Here are two points to bear in mind should you wish to try this approach.

First, there is no 'off-the-shelf' dispute resolution system: each one needs to be designed around the needs of the individual organization and its people. If, for example, you need to educate every member of the organization in dispute resolution, you might want to consider peer mediation as one of your stages of intervention. The use of peer meditation in a school, say, might be a good way to reduce bullying.

Secondly, while many organizations will be more than capable of designing their own dispute resolution systems, it can be useful to do it in collaboration with someone from outside. Not only is an outside view sometimes very useful, the 'outsider' may be able to deal with issues which are too sensitive to be handled by an 'insider'. An outsider can also absorb some of the resentment which accompanies any change in the status quo.

BEYOND DISPUTE RESOLUTION SYSTEMS: PARTNERING

Dispute prevention is the leading edge of ADR[15]. An example of this is *partnering* which has become increasingly widely used in recent years to cut the costs of conflict in major projects. Partnering, like all the best ADR, is no more than applied common sense. It involves establishing close working relationships between project management

---

[15] For more information about ADR in general, see my *Resolving Disputes Without Going to Court* (Century, 1995)

teams, partners, contractors, customers and generally anyone else involved before a project even begins, and fostering these relationships in such a way that the difficulties inevitable in any collaborative project do not end up in dispute and disaster.

The important elements in a partnering programme are:

- The partnering process is prepared and goes into operation as early as possible – as soon as the project is even mooted

- There is top-level commitment from all concerned at the outset and throughout

- Once the key players are decided, a joint workshop is held over several days to build working relationships, establish shared understanding of the project's key objectives, and identify potential areas of difficulty or dispute before they arise

- The workshop identifies 'champions' for the project who will take responsibility for maintaining the partnering process

- The formal product of the workshop is a *partnering charter*, produced by collaborative effort. It should cover everything: meeting the project designs; health and safety procedures; agreeing to use ADR should problems arise; agreeing to finish the project ahead of schedule and below estimate if possible

- The final element is follow-up meetings and constant monitoring and evaluation so that the lessons and benefits of partnering are continually reinforced, and any problems spotlighted before they escalate.

Some will say that good project management already does

this, and that is certainly true. But most project management is less systematic than it might be, and the volume of construction disputes reaching the courts, for example, suggests more can be done in terms of designing disputes *out* of projects right from their outset. The evidence for its benefits is in the results, as in the following example provided by the US Army Corps of Engineers, which is the arm of the American government responsible for many of North America's largest construction projects.

This was a construction project involving the replacement of a navigation lock on the Columbia River. It was an extremely complex project with a great deal of risk and uncertainty because of the geology of the site. The outcomes put down to the use of partnering included:

- No outstanding claims or litigation
- Engineering savings amounting to $1.8 million on a $34 million contract
- Cost growth of 3.3 per cent compared with typically 10 per cent on most major construction projects
- Project completed on schedule
- No time lost due to injuries
- A two-thirds reduction in letters and case-building paperwork relative to comparable projects.[16]

Partnering is undoubtedly the wave of the future for all the visionary lawyers and business people who resent the waste of time and cost spent fighting battles which need never have happened in the first place. Unfortunately, cost and inconvenience for one person is often profit and career for another, so you will not be surprised to learn that the legal profession, for example, is not overly enthusiastic about Alternative Dispute Resolution.

---

[16] This example is quoted in *Partnering*, a pamphlet in the US Army Corps of Engineers ADR Series, December 1991.

SKILL DEVELOPMENT

This concluding chapter on systems for preventing conflict is a little different from the others, in that there is no one skill to be identified and practised. It is perhaps fitting, though, that we should end with a chapter about a subject which involves all the people skills we have discussed and practised over the preceding pages.

For developing the skills of being a conflict preventer, I suggest you start close to home. *Again, complete this exercise with two others.*

Person A: identifies a situation in which he or she is regularly in conflict with someone: a partner, a child, a boss, a subordinate.

Person B: asks the questions which will analyse how and when this conflict happens.

Person C: designs and suggests alternative ways of doing things such that, if implemented, A's current conflicts could be prevented.

When complete, swap roles and go through the same process for **B** and **C**.

Summary

Someone once wrote acidly of 'systems so perfect that nobody needs to be good'.

It is a useful reminder that at the end of the day there is no substitute for decent behaviour by individuals. So I refer you back to the quotation from Robert Fulhum in the Introduction:

Most of what I really need to know about how to live, and what to do, and how to be, I learned in kindergarten. Wisdom was not at the top of the graduate school mountain, but there in the sandbox at nursery school. These are the things I learned: share everything; play fair; don't hit people; put things back where you found them; clean up your own mess; don't take things that aren't yours; say you're sorry when you hurt somebody; wash your hands before you eat . . .'

PERFECT RELAXATION

Elaine Van Der Zeil

Everyone is talking about stress these days and most people experience its negative symptoms from time to time. What is stress? How does it affect the way we live today? More importantly, how can learning to relax – both physically and mentally – help you to turn your challenges into triumphs?

Perfect Relaxation contains a wealth of strategies to help you take and keep control of your life and your stress levels.

- Understanding what stresses you
- Physical relaxation exercises
- Improving your sleep patterns
- Feeling positive about yourself
- Asserting your needs with others
- Sharing the load
- Managing your time and organizing yourself better
- Switching off
- Questionnaires and personal stress-beating plans

£5.99

ISBN 0–09–970531–1

PERFECT ASSERTIVENESS

Jan Ferguson

Perfect Assertiveness helps you to understand more about assertiveness and its importance as a life skill. The book shows you the difference between assertiveness and aggression, and teaches you to understand more about yourself, the possibilities of change and the potential for improvement in personal, social, family and workplace relationships.

- What does assertiveness really mean?
- Non-assertive behaviour and its results
- What's in it for you?
- You're in charge
- Learn to be your own best friend
- Moving on, letting go
- Handling conflict
- Being an assertive customer
- Setting boundaries and saying 'no'
- Steps to becoming more assertive

£5.99

ISBN 0–09–971051–X

PERFECT EXECUTIVE HEALTH

Dr Andrew Melhuish

The rapidly changing workplace, the results of the recession and the speed of technological innovation have combined to put those who are in work under fiercer pressures than ever before. Executives and managers suffer from many stress related health disorders which, as this book shows, can often be rectified by a more balanced lifestyle and sensible diet and exercise programmes. Dr Melhuish also examines many of the symptoms and diseases commonly affecting people in the workplace, and surveys both traditional medical treatment and more unorthodox practices such as homeopathy, hypnotherapy, acupuncture and cognitive therapy.

- Survival of the fittest
- From caveman to computer
- The chemical menace
- Managing your stress
- Lifestyle is the key
- When work makes you sick
- What is the alternative?
- The balancing act
- Moderation is the answer

£5.99

ISBN 0–09–917582–7

PERFECT EMPOWERMENT

Sarah Cook & Steve Macaulay

Empowerment, one of the most important business concepts of the 1990s, is a technique for improving customer and employee satisfaction. It involves pushing responsibility and authority for decisions affecting the workplace downwards through the organization. Those people closest to the customer are thus enabled to deliver a higher level of customer satisfaction and enhance organizational performance.

Many organizations attempt to empower their employees, but not all are successful. This invaluable book shows how it should be done.

- What is empowerment?
- Planning for empowerment
- Leading the empowerment process
- Creating an empowered environment
- Training and development
- Empowerment through teamwork
- Empowerment in action

£5.99

ISBN 0–09–966981–1

PERFECT DECISIONS

Andrew Leigh

Everybody has to make decisions, and this book gives a wealth of tips and information on how to make them more effectively. So much in our lives and careers depends on taking the right turn when we are faced with a choice of actions: *Perfect Decisions* helps you to minimize the guesswork and demystifies the decision making process, giving you the confidence to weigh up the pros and cons and pick the best course of action either by yourself or as part of a group.

- Introduction to decision making
- Problem solving
- The decision process
- Deciding to decide
- Style and intuition
- Tools of the trade
- Group decision making
- Pitfalls, confidence and checklist

£5.99

ISBN 0–7126–5902–1